QUENTIN CRISP'S BOOK OF QUOTATIONS

QUENTIN CRISP'S

1000 OBSERVATIONS ON

BOOK OF QUOTATIONS

LIFE AND LOVE BY, FOR, AND ABOUT GAY MEN AND WOMEN

WITH INTRODUCTIONS BY QUENTIN CRISP

EDITED BY AMY APPLEBY

MACMILLAN PUBLISHING COMPANY · NEW YORK

COLLIER MACMILLAN PUBLISHERS · LONDON

The lines by W. H. Auden from "Dichtung und Wahrheit" (page 32), "Lullaby" (page 32), and "The More Loving One" (page 183) are used with the permission of Faber and Faber Ltd, Random House, Inc., and Edward Mendelson, William Meredith, and Monroe K. Spears, Executors of the Estate of W. H. Auden.

The quotations from Jonathan Katz and from the documents collected in his books *Gay American History* and *Gay/Lesbian Almanac* are used with his permission.

Grateful acknowledgment is made for permission to reprint from *The Gay Spirit: Myth and Meaning,* edited by Mark Thompson (New York: St. Martin's Press, Inc., 1987).

Macmillan Publishing Company
866 Third Avenue, New York, NY 10022
Collier Macmillan Canada, Inc.

Library of Congress Cataloging-in-Publication Data
Quentin Crisp's book of quotations: 1000 observations of life and
    love by, for, and about gay men and women/edited by Amy Appleby;
    [collected and] with introductions by Quentin Crisp.
        p.   cm.
    Includes index.
    ISBN 0-02-528801-6
    1. Gays—Quotations.   2. Homosexuality.   3. Quotations, English.
I. Crisp, Quentin.   II. Appleby, Amy.   III. Title: Book of quotations.
PN6084.G35Q46   1989
082'.08'664—dc20   89-12364   CIP

Macmillan books are available at special discounts for bulk purchases for sales promotions, premiums, fund-raising, or educational use. For details, contact:

Special Sales Director
Macmillan Publishing Company
866 Third Avenue
New York, NY 10022

Designed by Beth Tondreau Design/Jane Treuhaft

10 9 8 7 6 5 4 3 2 1

PRINTED IN THE UNITED STATES OF AMERICA

CONTENTS

INTRODUCTION

P eople are neither heterosexual nor homosexual; they are merely sexual.

This has, presumably, been their nature from the beginning of human history, but attitudes toward this unpleasant fact have changed drastically from time to time and from one tribe to another. As in the studies of medicine and of astronomy, so in the matter of being gay, ideas have altered more rapidly in the past century than in all of previous recorded time. I have lived through the last eighty of these years of bewildering change, and in spite of all the terror and all the disillusionment would still maintain that the situation for homosexual men and women has improved.

Perhaps I take this sanguine view because I was born in England, which is such a thin-lipped island, and grew up in the suburbs of London, where it was not known that sex of any kind was here to stay. Beyond those neat front lawns, behind those carefully drawn curtains, it was hoped that if no one mentioned the beastly thing, it would go away. I never heard even the most oblique allusion to any of the more adventurous forms of carnality until I was at least twenty years old. My various oddities of appearance and behavior were deemed merely to be an irritating method of drawing attention to myself. Had I been born sixty years later and in another country, at least my problem would have been recognized even if it had been greeted with disapproval.

The sexual explosion that has recently burst upon us was caused by the fact that ever since the first Beatle twanged the first note on his guitar, money has fallen into the hands of the young. Until then juveniles were paupers; I can vouch for this statement from experience. As a child I was a dear little thing, a sort of toy for adults to play with, until I reached the age of ten. Then, when this flagrant imposture could not be maintained a moment longer either by me or by my mother, an angry silence reigned until I reluctantly agreed to be classified as a doubtful and doubting adult. I then received the equivalent of a modern fifty cents. I could not protest; I could not march; I could not buy or ride a motorbike; I could not get drunk or take drugs. I wasn't too good to do any of these things; I was too poor. My parents could see that I was miserable but at least I was quiet.

Now adolescents have money and, therefore, they have power. The world panders to them; there is a teenage market. Before this came into being I do not think that any manufacturer could have predicted what its principal wares would be, but now we know. They are skintight clothes and gramophone records. These weird products are, of course, only the outward and visible signs of an inward and carnal disgrace. They are the trappings of unbridled sensuality. The young have always wanted more sexual freedom than their parents thought was good for them and have usually cared less about a career than their elders would wish. Now they have their way. Getting on is out; getting off is in.

Inevitably, once sex in general could be mentioned more frequently and more crudely, it was not long before kinky sex also became a subject for contemplation and discussion.

In spite of this, caution should be exercised before assuming that we have entered a permissive society. Fundamentally, there is no such thing. A society is a large group of people who think they have something in common and who know that it is by the recognition and promotion of their homogeneity that they survive. Their communal life depends on the invention of a set of rules that inevitably limits the activities of its members—that name, condemn, and even punish those who commit what are in their judgment antisocial acts.

What we now endure is not so much an age of permissiveness as one of outspokenness. This minor revolution has affected our attitude toward sex more conspicuously than toward any other aspect of human behavior precisely because, until the sixties, it was the subject about which the least was said—in public, anyway.

Viewed in the hideous arc light that became focused upon it, homosexuality appeared at first to be primarily a masculine phenomenon. This was because, until very recently, though women talked more than men, they shouted very much less. It was therefore the conversation of men that was more often heard and more seriously heeded. Women were thought to concern themselves principally with their immediate surroundings, their families, and their friends, while men seemed to have few friends and to ignore their families completely; they concentrated upon their relationships with the world.

Historically, lesbian friendships are characterized not only by their longevity but also by a dignity so often lacking in male relationships. The union of Miss Stein and Miss Toklas is a perfect example. Can there ever have been a love so well known and yet so discreet?

In the hope of obtaining what they consider to be their rights, many women have discarded some of the more extreme symbols of femininity. In the minds of some people this has led to a misunderstanding. I have even heard the opinion expressed that lesbianism is a political movement. This idea is, of course, founded on the misconception that all homosexual women are mannish, that they look like Miss Stein or, at the very least, like Radclyffe Hall. This is a mirror image of the notion that all gay men are effeminate. Both these ideas are false, but they are maintained against all evidence to the contrary because they are tidy.

In England, before some of the laws of England condemning all forms of homosexual activity were repealed, a certain amount of market research into the subject was undertaken by the government. Women armed with clipboards went from door to door asking astonished housewives for their opinions about homosexuality. Early in each interview they were asked this question: "If you were told that you were about to meet a homosexual man, what kind of person would you expect to see?" Almost without exception the reply was, "Oh, you know. Someone a bit actorish—wearing bright colors and so on." Later on they were asked if they knew any gay men. If they did, they were asked what these boys looked like. To this query the answer more often than not was "Just like anybody else."

The traditional image of homosexual men and women persists only because it makes them easier to recognize and, consequently, easier to control.

With bowed head, I must confess that in my youth I too made the same ridiculous assumptions as the rest of the world. As I strolled about London the only homosexual boys that I saw or, at least, was sure that I saw were what in those days were called the fairies or pansies. From then on I either lived at home in a numbed trance of inertia or in lively misery among these obvious members of my tribe.

If our changing world could be described sexually, I would say it was becoming more masculine. In homosexual terms this means that lesbians—nay, that all women—are becoming more butch and that gay men are moving further and further from their old-fashioned camp appearance and manner. This latter trend has become so marked that in Chicago there are bars that quite shamelessly designate themselves as gay but on the walls of which hang notices warning patrons that the management takes exception to the slightest whiff of cologne or the faintest glint of precious stones. This new form of discrimination is a manifestation of another unalterable law, which states that if one group of people envies another, given the least opportunity, it will imitate the worst characteristics of the species it admires.

Gay men imitate the real world. What else can they imitate? Now that traditional notions of femininity have disappeared from the real world, they have disappeared from the gay world as well. So inevitably and possibly against its will, the homosexual community apes its environment. It goes beyond eschewing femininity; it shuns anything that might be called finesse.

In a time outworn, homosexual affairs were conducted as though they were quasi-heterosexual. There used to be at least a token wooing, a whirlwind courtship, even a minuscule trace of chivalry lavished on the nymph by the satyr. Now in this inner world, as in the outer one that threatens it, delicacy is dead. Sex is no longer a means by which one human being expresses his interest in or admiration for another. Where once there was romance, there is now nothing more edifying than that gross pooling of primitive urges that used merely to be the pastime of English public school boys.

For a while the epicene landscape in which we now find ourselves seemed to be a haven in which homosexuality could flourish. If heterosexuals were going to admit and even explore the androgynous attributes of their natures, it looked as though there might be at least an uneasy truce between them and the homosexual population—a chance for a tentative movement by society's outcasts toward the heart of the world. I sincerely imagined that the exiles wanted to come home. As I like people and am indifferent to their sex, this trend was especially welcome to me. Alas, it was short-lived; the tide has ebbed.

When I was really young I lived alone, and I was very lonely. And I would go and sit in a café in the hope that the waitress would speak to me. But after a bit you meet people, and through them you meet other people. In fact, up until about the age of twenty-five, most gay men and women are very glad to find others of their tribe at gay clubs. After the age of twenty-five I think you have to say, "Well, this is my life, and I've got to learn to live it without community." Those who try to invent a gay community only put themselves at a greater distance from the world. If you sink your individuality into a group identity, you will end up in the same prison that you were in when your mother said, "Why don't you cut your hair?"

The so uncivil rights movement has put an abrupt end to any hope of minorities being absorbed into the mainstream of humanity. The impatience of the species is at the root of this reversal of fortune. Anger begets anger. It is in the very nature of integration that you cannot fight for it—you can only wait. If you sue for integration, you place yourself in the same position as a suitor who asks, "Do you really love me?" The answer is almost certain to be an irritable "Okay, I love you. Now will you sit down and shut up?" What good is that?

At first I was shocked by what seemed to me a strategic error on the part of the would-be social reformers, and I was foolish enough to voice my misgivings. I was very soon made reluctantly to realize that if the gay community ever wished to enter the real world, it no longer does so. There is a movement afoot that those who like long words will one day term "reghettoization." This is easily recognizable as a subsection of the well-known ideal of being separate but equal. I fear that this goal may be a mirage. As the famous playwright Donna Severin says, "If they could just get over their heterophobia, all would be well."

Thus, in varying degrees, tolerance of homosexuality by the straight world and by gay men and women of one another is offered and withdrawn, accepted and rejected with bewildering rapidity as the decades rush past us.

It seems infinitely worthwhile and even urgent to try to record all these fascinating vicissitudes of relationship, all these shifts of moral emphasis that have disturbed our lives, but how is it best to be done? An abstruse philosophical tome will only ever be read by philosophers. To the average person some less laborious method must be found in which to present this eternal problem. What better way can there be than to compile, in an indexed and easily accessible form, the ideas on this subject, of people throughout the ages on both sides of the fence, expressed in their own words?

This is not, however, a joke book, nor is it an anthology of aphorisms—of ugly truths prettily phrased. This may surprise some potential readers who think of epigrams and poetry as the everyday speech of a certain category of gay men. In these pages can be heard both elegant and crude exclamations of disbelief or contempt or sheer panic from the unenlightened. Some of these express a genuine moral indignation; others are only the voice of a society determined to preserve itself at all costs from a force that it considers subversive but that in reality is, at its worst, iconoclastic and, at its least harmful, merely sterile and frivolous. From within the stockade come occasional cries of mourning, darkening growls of rage, and elsewhere, considered opinions from the gay community about its human environment and about itself.

Q.C.

QUENTIN CRISP'S BOOK OF QUOTATIONS

ART AND LITERATURE

The Bible tells us that "to the making of books there is no end." How appallingly true this is! Nevertheless, in an effort to appear broad-minded, the world now objects to censorship of any kind. The result of total artistic freedom is shows like Oh! Calcutta! and most of the books written about the gay scene by homosexual men.

Until recently gay literature was almost always defensive and sentimental. A prime example of this kind of writing was The Well of Loneliness. However much admiration one feels for Miss Hall, it cannot be denied that this is a very poor novel largely written in exclamatory prose. Nowadays, wallowing in the new freedom, we are drenched with a torrent of books that are little more than dreary catalogs of the author's sexual encounters, frequently described without taste or humor. Gay writers share with other minorities the problem of a too acute sensitivity to their image as a species. As soon as Mr. Poitier appeared on the screen, it seemed that there could never be a movie about a thoroughly unpleasant black man. It is a relief to see that that ludicrous state of affairs has now passed. In England there was an intermittent outcry against all characterization of homosexual men as effeminate. This was equally absurd.

Of course the world contains a large number of gay men and women who appear to themselves and all who know them to be just like real people. They form relationships as boring as a siege and lead contented, *uneventful lives, but the actions of such people can never be made into interesting reading matter.*

Minorities have to accept the fact that most books and all plays are about individuals coping with stress. After all, the Danish royal family has never tried to suppress Hamlet.

As far as I know—and, with bowed head, I admit that I am not well read—the only work that deals with a large assortment of homosexual men and women is Mr. Proust's, and that is because, in respect of them, he had no ax to grind.

We must all learn to accept that literature is not propaganda; it is simply anything memorable for the way it is written. Mr. Fierstein was delighted to hear that when asked if I thought Torch Song Trilogy *was a triumph for gay theater, I said, "No, it is a triumph for Mr. Fierstein."*

Those unnatural crimes and vile affections, which are most scandal-
ous at present, and carefully concealed, or most severely punished,
were openly avowed among the Greeks and Romans, even in their
politest ages; and their most elegant and celebrated poets have defiled
their compositions by the mention of such detestable amors, without
any expressions of abhorrence, or even of disapprobation; nay, often
in a way, which sanctions them, and almost wins the unwary reader
to palliate, or even approve them!

THOMAS SCOTT
English theologian, 1423–1500

[On Shakespeare]

Nay, e'en our bard, Dame Nature's darling child,
Felt the strange impulse, and his hours beguiled
In penning sonnets to a stripling's praise,
Such as would damn a poet now-a-days.

ANONYMOUS
English poet, 1833
From "Don Leon," a purported
autobiographical poem of Byron's life

When you read these, I, that was visible, am become invisible,
Now it is you, compact, visible, realizing my poems, seeking me,
Fancying how happy you were, if I could be with you, and become
      your lover;
Be it as if I were with you. Be not too certain but I am now with you.

WALT WHITMAN
American poet, 1819–1892

There is no such thing as a moral or an immoral book. Books are well written, or badly written. That is all.

OSCAR WILDE
Irish writer, 1854–1900

I never travel without my diary. One should always have something sensational to read in the train.

OSCAR WILDE
Irish writer, 1854–1900
From *The Importance of Being Earnest*

The books that the world calls immoral books are books that show the world its own shame.

OSCAR WILDE
Irish writer, 1854–1900
From *The Picture of Dorian Gray*

Knowledge came to me through pleasure, as it always does, I imagine. I was nearly sixteen when the wonder and beauty of the old Greek life began to dawn on me. . . . I began to read Greek eagerly for the love of it all, and the more I read the more I was enthralled.

OSCAR WILDE
Irish writer, 1854–1900
From *Lord Arthur Savile's Crime*

If ever there was a writer whose prayer to posterity might well have been "Read my works and let my life alone," it was Oscar [Wilde].

GEORGE BERNARD SHAW
Irish playwright/critic, 1856–1950

This love is misunderstood and despised, persecuted, and misinterpreted as nothing else in the world! . . . They murder our love—and it lives. They strangle our cry—and the future resounds with it! They have murdered my books. But my books will live. . . . Another judgment will be spoken by a brighter and better future. When, no one knows. But it is the only one I accept.

JOHN HENRY MACKAY
Scottish poet/writer, 1864–1933

The homosexual theme is common today in Continental fiction. The English-reading public accepts Gide and Proust with a certain complacent wonder—"How different from the home life of our own dear Queen."

ROBERT MORSS LOVETT
American educator/author, 1870–1956

It has always been my belief, or prejudice if you will, that explorations into the field of abnormal sexual psychology were better left to the scientific world and not forced upon the public.

SIDNEY WHIPPLE
American critic, 1938

[When asked during an interview how she might change the theme of her novel *Gentlemen Prefer Blondes* in view of the changing morals of the sixties, replied]

Gentlemen Prefer Gentlemen

ANITA LOOS
American novelist/screenwriter, 1893–1981

And I'll stay off Verlaine too; he was always chasing Rimbauds.

> DOROTHY PARKER
> American writer/humorist, 1893–1967

In Elizabethan England, where young boys played all the feminine roles on the stage, the device of having a boy playing the romantic role of a girl disguised as a boy fall in love with a man had almost infinite possibilities of amusement for the court and the crowd alike. At other times groups of writers, artists, musicians, and men and women related to the theater have cultivated bisexuality out of a delight with personality, regardless of race or class or sex.

> MARGARET MEAD
> American anthropologist, 1901–1978

[Comment regarding his homoerotic nude portraits of black Moroccan boys]

The Corsican boys, in the late 1930s, were not everyone's cup of tea. *I* find nudes of girls in black stockings singularly unappetizing.

> CECIL BEATON
> British photographer/writer/designer,
> 1902–1980

Nobody will believe me, of course, but Diaghilev did not know anything about dancing. His real interest in ballet was sexual. He could not bear the sight of Danilova and would say to me, "Her tits make me want to vomit." Once when I was standing next to him at a rehearsal for *Apollo,* he said, "How beautiful." I agreed, thinking that he was referring to the music, but he quickly corrected me: "No, no. I mean Lifar's ass, it is like a rose."

> GEORGE BALANCHINE
> American choreographer, 1904–1983

[Homosexuals are] indistinguishable from the straight man, except that they have more sensibility and they are more inclined to be good artists.

> TENNESSEE WILLIAMS
> American playwright, 1912–1983

He [Stephen Crane] now began a novel about a boy prostitute. . . . It was going to be called *Flowers of Asphalt* and was to be "longer than anything he had done." But Hamlin Garland, when Crane read him some of it, was horrified and begged him to stop. . . . The manuscript has not been traced.

> JOHN BERRYMAN
> American poet/author, 1914–1972

[Comment regarding the Oscar]

That naked little man tells the whole fuckin' world you're a big success.

> ROCK HUDSON
> American actor, 1925–1985

By the end of the year 2000 the whole world will be homosexual!

> FEDERICO FELLINI
> Italian writer/director
> Shouted by a transvestite at the end of the
> film *La Dolce Vita*, 1960

[*Victim*] was the first film in which a man said "I love you" to another man. I wrote that scene in. I said, "There's no point in half-measures. We either make a film about queers or we don't."

DIRK BOGARDE
English actor, 1961

You wouldn't expect me to only make films with gay themes because I am gay?

RAINER WERNER FASSBINDER
German film director, 1946–1982

The list of homosexuals in the theater is long, distinguished and international. It is also self-perpetuating.

The New York Times
1963

Arthur Miller is the only major playwright since World War II who had not been associated with homosexuality. He is also the only Jew.

WILLIAM GOLDMAN
American writer/screenwriter, 1969

If a swamp alligator could talk, it would sound like Tennessee Williams.

REX REED
American journalist/critic, 1972

If you are doing a drama or a comedy or a talk show about homosexuality, you have an obligation to do your homework and free yourself from the myths.

GAY ACTIVISTS ALLIANCE AND
NATIONAL GAY TASK FORCE
1973

I won't play lesbians, honey. Not this kid.

JANE WYMAN
American actress, 1976

I didn't want to play a lesbian at that time. Not very many women played recognizable lesbian roles in 1968, and that had a bearing on my decision. Now, of course, I think that the truth is filtering down to all of us, but I still don't think I'd play the part.

[Comments regarding her turning down the title role in the film *The Killing of Sister George,* directed by Robert Aldrich]

ANGELA LANSBURY
American actress, 1976

Don't play no faggots.

[Advice to actor and friend Perry King, regarding his acceptance of the role of a gay man in the film *A Different Story,* 1978]

SYLVESTER STALLONE
American actor/director, 1978

I'm obviously a homosexual writer with hardly a woman in his books.

WILLIAM S. BURROUGHS
American novelist, 1978

The Children's Hour by Lillian Hellman was rumored to be a leading contender for the Pulitzer Prize for 1934–35, but it was bypassed, presumably because it dealt with charges of lesbianism. . . . Its supporters denounced the Pulitzer Committee for cowardice and censorship.

ABE LAUFE
American writer/historian, 1978

Gay people don't need any more screen martyrs.

HOWARD ROSENMAN
American film producer, 1979

There has turned out to be an advantage in the fact that [*The Naked Civil Servant*] was made for television. If it had been a movie, it would have been advertised as having a homosexual theme, and nobody would have seen it except gay men—oh, and liberals wishing to be seen going into and coming out of the cinema.

QUENTIN CRISP
English writer/critic, 1979

Isn't it peculiar that in a movie [*La Cage aux Folles*] that celebrates a long-lasting lovers' marriage, we never once see the lovers kiss?

DAVID ANSEN
American critic, 1980

Why couldn't this collection be locked up again, at least for several decades? . . . Eleanor Roosevelt was a great woman and her effusively affectionate letters should be removed until the year 2000.

[Spoken to the library director of the National Archives regarding the love letters of Eleanor Roosevelt and Lorena Hickock. The Archives ruled against suppression of the letters and Ms. Faber grudgingly used them in her biography of Hickock.]

DORIS FABER
American biographer, 1980

[Regarding his play on AIDS, *The Normal Heart*]

This is not a play about measles.

LARRY KRAMER
American playwright, 1980s

At the heart of *The Normal Heart,* the element that gives this powerful political play its essence, is love—love holding firm under fire, put to the ultimate test, facing and overcoming our greatest fear: death.

JOSEPH PAPP
American producer/director, 1980

It's up to gay writers to correct history and to create valid, positive characters and even stereotypes.

BARRY SANDLER
American playwright, 1980s

He [Little Richard] was like nothing anyone had ever seen. Before "King of the Blues," he announced himself. "And the Queen too!" His lyrics to "Tutti-Frutti" had to be cleaned up before a Hollywood company agreed to record it, but when they were, and they did, he became the King and Queen of Rock 'n' Roll besides.

ANDREW HOLLERAN
American literary critic, 1980s

A gay poem is one that's sexually attracted to other poems.

WILLIAM BARBER
American poet, 1980s

Hollywood's latest crime against humanity in general and homosexuals in particular is a dumb creep show called *Partners*—stupid, tasteless and homophobic, this sleazy, superficial film implies that gay cops cannot be trusted to work with straight cops because they might fall in love with them.

REX REED
American critic, 1982

According to this movie [*Personal Best*], lesbianism is just something you catch in the locker room, like athlete's foot.

REX REED
American critic, 1982

The gay tradition in poetry is a substantial one, more so in cultures other than the Western. The Greek, Persian, Arabic and Japanese cultures all produced openly homoerotic verse, whereas in Europe, the fervid morbidities of Christianity led to the suppression of gay writing, or at best its concealment by the alteration of gender—a sort of literary sexchange.

IAN YOUNG
Canadian poet/writer/translator, 1982

Years ago, when I was editor [of the gay newspaper the *Advocate*], we had planned to drop those nasty classifieds to make the paper more acceptable to large national advertisers and, we thought, to attract more bourgeois subscribers. The slightest bit of market research proved that any such move would have been a disaster.

JOHN PRESTON
American writer, 1983

I think gay playwrights should be able to use their truths. A gay playwright can write about gay people and be just as universal as a straight person.

JOHN GLINES
American producer, 1983

For homosexuals, [the play *La Cage aux Folles*], even more than *Torch Song Trilogy*, is the Broadway legitimization of their modus vivendi, all the way from respectably bourgeois to outrageously transvestite, via a budget of $5 million.

JOHN SIMON
American critic, 1983

Critics are forever discovering homosexual references in my plays where they don't exist.

EDWARD ALBEE
American playwright, 1983

It would be easy to extend the list of gay lives that have been misappropriated and rewritten, from Sappho to Willa Cather, from Socrates to Herman Melville. It is time to reclaim some of these lives.

ROBERT K. MARTIN
American writer/critic, 1983

Every year, they publish thousands of non-gay books which they know have no hope of commercial success, and yet they are reluctant to move further into the gay market than to publish Gore Vidal and Truman Capote. . . . Gay literature is moving into our own hands.

NORMAN LAURILLA
American bookseller/activist, 1984

As I stood pressed against the railings of some dim London square with a stranger's hand at my throat or my crotch or both, another member of the gang would whisper, "But he's an artist. I seen him in Chelsea." Immediately the grip on my person would loosen and, in a shaken voice, my aggressor would say, "I didn't know."

QUENTIN CRISP
English writer/critic, 1984

Now there is a certain cinema in London where it is said that all the films shown have a "Q" certificate (no normal person may be admitted to any part of this program unless accompanied by a homosexual).

QUENTIN CRISP
English writer/critic, 1984

In Japan in the 1970s, Mishima was deliberately forgotten. But now nationalism is stronger and the gay liberation movement is moving and growing. So Mishima is a cultural hero to many groups, including gay men and right-wing military fans. Also those who love his poetry and literature.

NAGASA OSHIMA
Japanese film director, 1984

Because homosexual men are pathologically incapable of making love with their friends or making friends of their lovers, it is not possible to write a satisfactory play about their world. The dialogue can only be midday gossip or moonlit grunts. A dramatist tends to sink into the sentimentality of *The Boys in the Band* or lapse into mere pornography.

QUENTIN CRISP
English writer/critic, 1985

As for overt homosexuality in pre-1960 films, it was not attempted and not possible. Sonnets have fourteen lines. You wrote sonnets then and there was never an extra or an odd line . . . but subtexts did occasionally insert themselves.

GORE VIDAL
American novelist, 1985

According to Steven [Spielberg], middle America simply would not sit still for me on top and Shug on bottom, so we made it less explicit. This way we won't offend anyone.

[Commenting on the lesbian love scene in *The Color Purple*]

WHOOPI GOLDBERG
American actress/writer, 1985

[Regarding his play *Torch Song Trilogy*]

Like a gaudy East Indian purse; outrageous in color, embroidered in cliché design, the worth of these plays lies ultimately in the tiny mirrors woven into the fabric wherein we catch our reflections. Perhaps you'll see a little of yourself on the phone with Arnold's "Why don't you love me anymore?" call.

HARVEY FIERSTEIN
American playwright, 1985

Although *All About Eve* is a wonderfully witty movie, do not use any of its lines in life—or in a [gay] bar.

T. R. WITOMSKI
American writer, 1985

Try to calmly accept the fact that Baryshnikov is straight. Don't take an overdose every time you see him photographed with a woman.

TONY LANG
American humorist, 1985

Keep in mind that history has given us a great many illustrious homosexuals and it is fairly safe to assume that most of them were a little bit—well, *different* from everybody else. It's doubtful, for instance, that when Michelangelo walked down the street, people turned to each other and said, "There goes another gay muralist. See? He's carrying his brushes on the left."

TONY LANG
American humorist, 1985

Homosexuals have commonly been treated shabbily in detective fiction—vilified, pitied, at best patronized. This was neither fair nor honest. When I sat down to write *Fadeout* in 1967 I wanted to write a good, compelling whodunit, but I also wanted to right some wrongs.

JOSEPH HANSEN
American novelist, 1985

Virginia Woolf exemplifies the problem of deciding who is a lesbian writer.

MARGARET CRUIKSHANK
American educator/writer, 1986

I have encountered clients who enter therapy questioning their adequacy as lovers, women, and indeed as lesbians because they find themselves unable to measure up to standards set by the heroines of post-liberation lesbian romantic novels.

LAURA S. BROWN
American psychologist/sexologist, 1986

I've never fully trusted a gay man who doesn't love Judy Garland.

GREGG HOWE
American writer, 1986

They're not effeminate either, some of them are really manly and you'd never dream they were queer. Not from the look of them. But I can always tell 'cos they've *all* got LPs of Judy Garland.

JOE ORTON
English playwright, 1933–1967
Spoken by a fellow Orton picked up once

The opera queen . . . is a civic institution, like the cop on the corner. He serves an important function, like that served at the gladiatorial games by Caesar's thumb. No singer who hasn't won her faction among opera queens can be said to have arrived, regardless of how often she's been on the "Johnny Carson Show."

IVAN MARTINSON
American journalist/critic, 1986

One of the rare things about being gay is that you can write about things that weren't discussed before fifty years ago. Only since then, which is a rather short time, have people been in any way open about homosexuality, and there is still a lot more to be discussed.

EDMUND WHITE
American novelist/essayist, 1988

I like the word *gay*, though I think of myself more as *queer*. I believe the strength in my work comes from that perspective—my being an outsider.

HOLLY HUGHES
American playwright, 1988

If you want to know who the oppressed minorities in America are, you simply look at who gets their own shelf in the bookstore. A black shelf, a women's shelf, and a gay shelf.

ARMISTEAD MAUPIN
American novelist, 1988

I think it's largely because of the gay content that my plays are produced.

LANFORD WILSON
American playwright, 1988

People often ask, was Shakespeare gay? No, he was beyond being gay. He wasn't even bisexual. He was everything with equal passion.

IAN MCKELLAN
English actor, 1988

I find that a lot of gay writing today is more specifically directed at gay people. We're under a siege. Gay artists are trying to create a protected place where we can still have some pride.

LANFORD WILSON
American playwright, 1988

Traditionally men's room walls have been a major outlet for homosexuals to express themselves directly and honestly. The writing on men's room walls is among the finest this country has produced.

BOYD MCDONALD
American writer, 1988

[Comment regarding negative press resulting from Mariette Pathy Allen's use of her New York State Council on the Arts grant to fund a photographic study of transvestites]

We fund art, not politics.

KITTY CARLISLE HART
American actress/arts administrator
Director, New York State Council on the
Arts, 1988

If Michelangelo were a heterosexual, the Sistine Chapel would have been painted basic white and with a roller.

RITA MAE BROWN
American writer, 1988

BEAUTY

A part from the Greeks of classical times, whom history presents to us as having been preoccupied with physical beauty to a nauseating degree, no society ever set more store by bodily perfection than modern Americans. At the moment thin is beautiful. When I was last in Los Angeles, where glamour grows on trees, the women talked of nothing but what they refrained from eating. It was in vain that I told them that I had never heard a man praise a girl because she was skinny.

Though ideals of loveliness change from generation to generation and with each nationality, one factor is constant: Beauty is in the eye of the possessor. As Mr. Beaton, the British photographer, said of Fräulein Dietrich, "What does it matter whether or not she is the most beautiful woman in the world? She feels beautiful enough to convince anybody," and she herself said, concerning her famous legs, "It is not that they are particularly good; it is just that I know what to do with them."

The most beautiful woman who ever lived was Brigitte Helm. She was a star of any number of German silent movies (the only one existing is called Metropolis). Miss Helm was invented by a man called Fritz Lang. He filled in the space on the bridge of her nose with old string and sealing wax and painted it over. And once he'd shown her pictures of herself, that's the way she looked forever after. So in the broadest sense of all, beauty is consciousness. As Garbo said, "I told them I was beautiful, and they believed me." Sadly, Marilyn Monroe remained forever a victim because there was no one there to tell her who she was.

Good looks are their own reward. Whatever joy they hold, they bestow on their owner. To their admirers they promise nothing. The pretty woman and the handsome man are at no pains to please their lovers because they need no reassurance. The superficial admiration of the general public is enough.

I have never been told what lesbians look for in one another's faces. As their relationships tend to last longer than those of gay men, I would expect them to search for hints of strength of character—of a capacity for loyalty. Many homosexual men, on the contrary, who require instant and constant gratification, are preoccupied either with purely sexual dimensions or with the most obvious and conventional type of handsomeness. They want a partner who is tall, blond, and blue-eyed and has a deep chest and a flat stomach. They demand these attributes less for their own sake than because they lend a fleeting triumph to the person who arrives with such an Adonis at the local bar—or more important, departs with him from it. It never occurs to such gay men that they might receive more attention from or even have a more uproarious romp with a potbellied, middle-aged man.

Perhaps it is because of this perpetual and misguided search for one of these Apollonian paragons that many male gay liaisons are so dangereuses—and so brief.

Really, the idea of being the cleverest, the handsomest, the bravest, and the boldest means you're simply the most beautiful person in the eyes of certain people for that year. You must look the way you want to look. I used to know a man who dressed in full Texas gear. And I said, "Why do you do this?" And he said, "I find I get laid because of my hat."

The problem with gay men who are into leather is often the same: they don't really mean it. I went to a club full of leather men in Washington. Now, if I'd been told when I was young that there was a tavern in the town where the brave and the cruel were gathered, I would have run all the way. I would have gone up to the largest and leatheriest *person and I would have said, "If you love me, kill the bartender." He probably wouldn't have done it. He'd be standing there, bristling with steel studs, talking about the ballet.*

Your clothes must tell the world who you are. That's the point of clothes. We wear clothes, and speak, and live in a certain way to bring ourselves nearer to the world. What else do we have? When appearance reflects style, it eliminates all the dead wood in human relationships. That is to say, no one ever talks to me about the weather.

Lovers look at none of the bodily charms of their favorites more than at their eyes, wherein dwells the secret of boyish virtues.

ARISTOTLE
Greek philosopher, 384 B.C.–322 B.C.

See, his beard is sprouting yet,
Beauty's fringes delicate;
Delicately through my heart
Passion's thrilling raptures dart.

IBN SARA
Arabian poet

Oh here's to the boy that is pale as snow,
    And to those with the color of honey:
I dote on them dark and I'll have them when tow
    And I love them when open and sunny.

I covet them fair and I don't mind them thin,
    I adore them as brown as a pebble:
But the best of the bunch have a rich olive skin
    And flashing black eyes like the devil.

STRATO
Greek writer, c. A.D. 2

Come bathe in the scented waters,
    And weave for us garlands bright;
For boys and wine won't stay for ever,
    And the grave offers no delight.

STRATO
Greek writer, c. A.D. 2

Labienus, each hair on your bosom that grows,
    On your arms, on your legs, with much trouble
You shave, and your belly's appurtenance shows
    Like a newly mown field with its stubble.
Thus blooming and sweet as the breath of the morn,
    Your mistress entwines you, fond boy,
But you've something behind, neatly shaven and shorn,
    That's scarcely a mistress's toy.

> MARTIAL
> Roman poet/epigrammatist, 40–104

It is frequently the case with young men [in the monastery] that even when rigorous self-restraint is exercised, the glowing complexion of youth still blossoms forth and becomes a source of desire to those around them. If, therefore, anyone is youthful and physically beautiful, let him keep his attractiveness hidden until his appearance reaches a suitable state.

Sit in a chair far from such a youth; in sleep do not allow your clothing to touch his but, rather, have an old man between you.

> ST. BASIL
> Early Church father, 330?–379?

Golden haired, fair of face, with a small white neck,
Soft-spoken and gentle—but why do I praise these singly?
Everything about you is beautiful and lovely; you have no imperfection,
Except that such fairness has no business devoting itself to chastity.

> HILARY THE ENGLISHMAN
> English poet, 1150?

Beautiful boy, flower fair,
Glittering jewel, if only you knew
That the loveliness of your face
Was the torch of my love.

HILARY THE ENGLISHMAN
English poet, 1150?

It passes from the eyes into the heart
In a split second. Thus all beauties may
Find by this means a wide and generous way;
And so, for countless men, desires start.

MICHELANGELO BUONARROTI
Italian sculptor/painter/architect/poet
1475–1564

His body was as straight as Circe's wand;
Jove might have sipt out nectar from his hand.
Even as delicious meat is to the taste,
So was his neck in touching, and surpast
The white of Pelops' shoulder: I could tell ye,
How smooth his breast was, and how white his belly,
And whose immortal fingers did imprint
That heavenly path with many a curious dint,
That runs along his back; but my rude pen
Can hardly blazon forth the loves of men,
Much less of powerful gods.

CHRISTOPHER MARLOWE
English poet/playwright, 1564–1593

When the young males of our species, brought up together, feel the force which nature begins to unfold in them, and fail to find the natural object of their instinct, they fall back on what resembles it. Often, for two or three years, a young man resembles a beautiful girl, with the freshness of his complexion, the brilliance of his coloring, and the sweetness of his eyes; if he is loved, it's because nature makes a mistake.

> VOLTAIRE
> French philosopher/scientist/writer
> 1694–1778

Those who are only aware of beauty in the female sex, and are hardly or not at all affected by beauty in *our* sex, have little innate feeling for beauty in art in a general and vital sense.

> JOHANN JOACHIM WINCKELMANN
> German art historian, 1717–1768

You are my Greek god, dear youth. I want to sleep with you, embrace you. When you bathe in Lake Thun, I stare at your magnificent body with the longing of a girl.

> HEINRICH VON KLEIST
> German playwright/poet/novelist,
> 1777–1811

His *voice* first attracted my attention, his *countenance* fixed it, and his *manners* attached me to him forever.

> LORD BYRON
> English poet, 1788–1824

Winds that breathe about, upon her
(Lines I do not dare)
Whisper, turtle, breathe upon her
That I find her fair.

> Angelina Grimké Weld
> American poet, 1805–1879

While they discuss I am silent, and go bathe and admire myself.
Welcome is every organ and attribute of me, and of any man hearty
    and clean,
Not an inch nor a particle of an inch is vile, and none shall be less
    familiar than the rest.

> Walt Whitman
> American poet, 1819–1892

You, proud curve-lipped youth, with brown sensitive face,
Why, suddenly, as you sat there on the grass, did you turn full upon
    me those twin black eyes of yours,
With gaze so absorbing, so intense, I a strong man trembled and was
    faint?

> Edward Carpenter
> English writer/activist, 1844–1929

Even men of the noblest possible moral character are extremely
susceptible to the influence of the physical charms of others.

> Oscar Wilde
> Irish writer, 1854–1900
> From *The Importance of Being Earnest*

"But was Narcissus beautiful?" said the pool.

"Who should know better than you?" answered the Oreads.

"Us he did ever pass by, but you he sought for, and would lie on your banks and look down at you, and in the mirror of your waters he would mirror his own beauty."

And the pool answered, "But I loved Narcissus because, as he lay on my banks and looked down at me, in the mirror of his eyes I saw ever my own beauty mirrored."

> OSCAR WILDE
> Irish writer, 1854–1900
> From *Poems in Prose*

Ethics, like natural selection, make existence possible. Aesthetics, like sexual selection, make life lovely and wonderful, fill it with new forms, and give it progress, and variety and change.

> OSCAR WILDE
> Irish writer, 1854–1900
> From *The Critic as Artist*

[From a letter to Lord Alfred Douglas, submitted as evidence at his trial for sodomy]

It is a marvel that those red rose-leaf lips of yours should have been made no less for the music of song than for the madness of kissing.

> OSCAR WILDE
> Irish writer, 1854–1900

My dear, you used to be quite a dish; now you're quite a tureen.

[To his lover, Alan Searle]

> SOMERSET MAUGHAM
> English novelist/playwright, 1874–1965

WIDOW: I have heard you do not like the fair sex.

CAPTAIN CONRAD: The fair sex? Which one is that?

> J. R. ACKERLEY
> English playwright, 1935
> From *The Prisoners of War*

A thing of beauty is a boy forever.

> CARL VAN VECHTEN
> American photographer/writer, 1880–1964

It's better to be looked over than overlooked.

> MAE WEST
> American actress/playwright, 1892–1980

I will love you whatever happens, even though you put on twenty
pounds or become afflicted with a moustache.

> W. H. AUDEN
> American poet, 1907–1973

Lay your sleeping head, my love,
Human on my faithless arm;
Time and fevers burn away
Individual beauty from
Thoughtful children . . .
But in my arms till break of day
Let the living creature lie,
Mortal, guilty, but to me
The entirely beautiful.

> W. H. AUDEN
> American poet, 1907–1973

My face looks like a wedding cake left out in the rain.

> W. H. AUDEN
> American poet, 1907–1973

Chekhov was probably gay. But he was very ill, and whether or not he practiced his sexual inclination . . . if you were to look at early pictures of him you would see that he was a very beautiful man with a very sensitive face that you were not likely to encounter among straight men.

> TENNESSEE WILLIAMS
> American playwright, 1912–1983

[Noel] Coward invented the concept of cool. And if his face suggested an old boot, it was unquestionably hand-made.

> KENNETH TYNAN
> English critic, 1927–1980

They photographed everyone to look as pretty as possible and, having no competition, I won.

> JOE ORTON
> English playwright, 1933–1967

When you think of a bombshell, you think of Monroe or Mansfield, you don't think of a three-hundred-pound man. People like to be shocked.

> DIVINE
> American actor, 1946–1988

[From his description of a New York bathhouse]

At any time you may witness couplings of white with black, beauty
with horror, aardvark with dinosaur, panda with pachyderm, skinny-
old-slate-gray-potbelly-bald with chubby-old-slate-gray-potbelly-bald,
heartbreakingly gentle with stimulatingly rugged—but always, para-
doxically, like with like.

NED ROREM
American composer, 1967

I wore makeup at a time when even on women eye shadow was sinful.
Many a young girl in those days had to leave home and go on the
streets simply in order to wear nail varnish.

QUENTIN CRISP
English writer/critic, 1968

Although I am not a Lesbian, I do share the normal human response
to whatever is attractive physically in either sex.

GORE VIDAL
American writer, 1968
Myra Breckinridge, in *Myra Breckinridge*

I saw Joan Crawford at the National Film Theatre. For a second she
saw me with those great alligator's eyes. It felt as though my innards
were being burned on the wall behind me. She was radioactive with
belief in herself.

QUENTIN CRISP
English writer/critic, 1979

Beauty is a complete waste of time: because without even knowing it, we still cringe in the shadow of classical ideals of beauty. The Greeks were mad about the human body—so much so, that during its heyday, Athens must have looked like an outfitter's window during a weavers' strike. But it was no help—not one of the great classical statues has the least physical individuality which would make it desirable or even interesting. So beauty you will never need.

QUENTIN CRISP
English writer/critic, 1979

The point of having a face is that it is something that other people recognize, and if you change it so as to make it something quite different, this is to my mind a great mistake. Once you've had your face lifted, you have to alter your entire past—you have to be careful not to remember who Greta Garbo is. I couldn't bear not to remember who Greta Garbo is.

QUENTIN CRISP
English writer/critic, 1979

One man's queen is another man's sweathog.

JONATHAN WILLIAMS
American poet, 1980s

It's the daylight you gotta watch out for. Face it, a thing of beauty is a joy till sunrise.

HARVEY FIERSTEIN
American playwright/actor, 1981
Arnold, in *Torch Song Trilogy*

Gay society, whether one likes it or not, is based very much on looks. A person's physique, not his personality, often attracts the initial response. When men first seek out other men they don't generally inquire, "Does he have a brilliant mind?" The presentation of one's flesh gets first notice.

> ROY F. WOOD
> American writer/activist, 1985

Don't augment a tan with anything from a bottle.

> TONY LANG
> American humorist, 1985

Don't wear anything made out of old parachutes.

> TONY LANG
> American humorist, 1985

Every primer on meeting new friends and winning lovers seems to intone *Be yourself.* I'm not sure that's such good advice. Better to go to a gay bar being the person you want to be.

> T. R. WITOMSKI
> American writer, 1985

If, "manners maketh man" as someone said,
Then he's the hero of the day
It takes a man to suffer ignorance and smile
Be yourself no matter what they say.

> STING (Gordon Matthew Sumner)
> English singer/musician/actor, 1987
> From his song about Quentin Crisp,
> "Englishman in New York"

The difference between gay males and straight males is that the former start a trend and the latter pick it up after it appears in the Avon Catalogue. Where do you think fashion designers get their ideas? Chasing queens around London to see what they're going to make out of the curtains next.

IAN LYNCH
American image consultant, 1988

COMING OUT

I n younger and happier days, coming out was a ritual performed by the daughters of rich and well-born or at least well-connected parents. The mothers of these girls took them to a series of fashionable gatherings in the hope that this social exposure would lead to matrimony.

Now coming out is a defiant gesture made by certain young men and women in the teeth of opposition from their parents, and at least one of its objects is to put an end forever to any discussion of marriage.

This may be considered a sign of great courage, especially in anyone who does not by his very nature bear the obvious physical stigmata of sexual ambiguity. It may also be deemed a foolish sacrifice if undertaken by the young or, indeed, by anyone who does not yet hold in his head a complete and immutable picture of his own identity. I have known a number of men who have changed sexual horses in midstream. If all such people reveal their guilty secret in adolescence, they may forfeit much of the parental support, general friendship, and civic honor that, if they say nothing, becomes their natural inheritance for the larger part of their lives.

Admitting to oneself that one is gay is not coming out nor, as some people seem to imagine, is the frequenting of gay bars, gay restaurants, or even gay parties. Coming out is allowing one's sin to be known beyond all shadow of doubt by people with whom one is associated in the real world.

What is often not recognized is that this debauch of self-revelation does not merely usher in a lifetime of sexual license; it carries with it an obligation to behave better than ever before and than everybody else. It has no effect whatsoever to state in lectures and in pamphlets that homosexual men and women inflict upon society no harm specifically related to their sexual preference; this fact has to be demonstrated. Coming out is like joining a regiment; a uniform is worn to remind the wearer as well as the rest of the world that he represents a group of people whose honor stands or falls by his individual behavior.

I myself was never compelled to make up my mind about these grave ethical issues. I never came out because I was never in.

I dare not tell it in words—not even in these songs.

> WALT WHITMAN
> American poet, 1819–1892

Publish my name and hang up my picture as that of the tenderest lover.

> WALT WHITMAN
> American poet, 1819–1892

Why do you suppose that Noel [Coward] or I never stuck our personal predilections down the public's throats? Because we know it would outrage them. Believe me, I know what I'm talking about. Don't put your head in a noose.

> SOMERSET MAUGHAM
> English novelist/playwright, 1874–1965

Indiscretion has always seemed to me one of the privileges of tact.

> NATALIE CLIFFORD BARNEY
> American author, 1876–1972

It is the first time in our English-speaking literary history that identified individuals, as opposed to fictional characters, have been treated as openly bisexual, capable of loving and relating to individuals of both sexes frankly and with the accent on both personality and sex. What is new is not bisexuality, but rather the widening of our awareness and acceptance of human capacities for sexual love.

> MARGARET MEAD
> American anthropologist, 1901–1978

Let me tell you something that Mae West said. She was asked about the men she was seen with in public. And she replied, "It's not the men you see me with, it's the men you don't see me with." That is true of everybody in public life.

CECIL BEATON
British photographer/writer/designer
1902–1980

DAVID FROST: Are you a homosexual?

TENNESSEE WILLIAMS: I cover the waterfront.

TENNESSEE WILLIAMS
American playwright, 1912–1983
From a television interview with
David Frost

Everybody knew I was a gay playwright. Many, many years ago *Time* was the first publication to spell it out, that I was homosexual. I didn't give a damn.

TENNESSEE WILLIAMS
American playwright, 1912–1983

Perhaps most actors are latent homosexuals and we cover it with drink. I was once a homosexual, but it didn't work.

RICHARD BURTON
Welsh actor, 1925–1984

I like to keep my secrets to myself, and I guess they will die with me.

ROCK HUDSON
American actor, 1925–1985

Okay, okay. If you're asking am I one, I'll go that route—good public relations. If it's good enough for Gore Vidal and Elton John, it's good enough for me. I am bisexual, happy and proud. A woman in every bed . . . and a man, too. Satisfied?

> ROCK HUDSON
> American actor, 1925–1985

If they know, they know. If they don't, they don't. Fuck 'em!

> ROCK HUDSON
> American actor, 1925–1985

Homosexuality shears across the spectrum of American life—the professions, the arts, business and labor. It always has. But today, especially in big cities, homosexuals are discarding their furtive ways and openly admitting, even flaunting, their deviation.

> *Life* magazine, 1964

Boys-R-Us

> American T-shirt slogan, 1970s

If I look it, I probably am.

> American T-shirt slogan, 1970s

From the beginning of the gay liberation movement, the Stonewall riots of June, 1969, the *Times* and other elements of the mass media have misunderstood just how traumatic and new and courageous is "coming out."

STUART BYRON
American writer, 1972

I came out of the closet at Columbia in 1946. The first person I told about it was Kerouac, 'cause I was in love with him. He was staying in my room up in the bed, and I was sleeping on a pallet on the floor. I said, "Jack, you know, I love you, and I want to sleep with you, and I really like men." And he said, "Oooooh, no . . ."

ALLEN GINSBERG
American poet, 1975

Let the bullets that rip through my brain smash through every closet door in the nation.

HARVEY MILK
American politician/activist, 1930–1978

Now Allen Ginsberg gets up before an audience of college students and talks about how he jacked off Peter Orlovsky last night, and they all cheer. Forty years ago they'd have been ridden out on a rail. So that is a terrific change.

WILLIAM S. BURROUGHS
American novelist, 1978

Charles Laughton played every kind of part but never a homosexual. People knew he was gay, but his public image never betrayed his private reality. So he was safe. I wasn't safe.

ROBERT LA TOURNEAUX
American actor, 1978

When people ring me up and say, "What shall I do? My mother doesn't understand," I say, "First of all, have you tried doing nothing? Have you tried saying nothing?" And if that doesn't work, I say, "Neither confirm or deny. Don't get in a conversation with your parents which leads them to imagine you will one day marry someone you have been to the pictures with three times. On the other hand, don't waltz down to breakfast with the words, 'Guess what?' Because this will only worry them."

QUENTIN CRISP
English writer/critic, 1979

I'm trying to speak to those people who feel the band always seems to be playing in another street, and who feel that they're mysteriously locked in their rooms. And when I say, "The door is not locked, go to where the band is playing," they say, "I haven't a thing to wear." Now, as I see it, you only have to wear your wonderful selves. And what I feel gives me the right to say it is that if I, who am nothing, who am nobody, have gotten to New York with my fare paid, anyone can do it.

QUENTIN CRISP
English writer/critic, 1979

My advice in general to gay people is simply to go on living your life as though you did not see any reason either to boast of or to conceal your life.

> QUENTIN CRISP
> English writer/critic, 1979

Ever since I had that interview in which I said I was bisexual it seems twice as many people wave at me in the streets.

> ELTON JOHN
> English musician, 1980s

Like many men, I too have had homosexual experiences and I am not ashamed.

> MARLON BRANDO
> American actor, 1980s

Most of us have struggled, for a time at least, against the realization of our gayness, and coming out is therefore a long and painful process. I fought my homosexuality for a long time.

> DENNIS ALTMAN
> Australian writer, 1980s

[Response to the question, "What is the word for *gay* in French?"]

We don't have one; we don't have a word because we don't have the thing itself. You know, I think the name is the most important aspect of the thing it names. I think what we call "coming out" for gay people is saying "I am gay." Nobody knows that you are gay until you say it—even if you are effeminate or show some outward signs that you are gay. It's not the same for, say, blacks, and the case is clearer here than it is for Jews: nobody will know that you are gay—perhaps not even yourself—unless you say it.

GUY HOCQUENGHEM
French activist, 1980s

During the heterosexual years it was rumored that I took on eight men at one time. During the lesbian years, it was rumored that I had orgies in which my daughter (aged eleven, twelve, thirteen) participated. For the full year after I came out, she was ostracized by her peers—only a few friends remained loyal (though remain loyal they did). She, as I, had been branded a pervert and a whore (take your pick).

MARCIA FREEDMAN
American feminist/activist, 1982

When Oscar Wilde "feasted with panthers," he was not, as some have suggested, seeking his own destruction; he was testing the limits of his own disguise.

ROBERT K. MARTIN
American writer/critic, 1983

Speaking for myself, in a way I did not anticipate a decade ago, the self-acceptance and public proclamation of "gay" has in some ways, in some contexts, made that category less important, less all-defining than it was when they still held it over me and us as an essential dirty secret of the soul.

JONATHAN KATZ
American historian, 1983

The attitudes of those with a preference for the same sex are no different in kind from those with preferences for different kinds of sexuality. I've been quite consistent on that. And as for discussing myself, that's not my style. I don't do that sort of thing. It's partly a matter of age and it's partly a matter of the world I come from. We don't do that. But I don't mind it when Henry Miller does, or Norman Mailer does, and I love it when Shelley Winters does! But it's just not for me.

GORE VIDAL
American writer, 1984

I managed to shift homosexuality from being a burden to being a cause. The weight lifted and some of the guilt evaporated.

QUENTIN CRISP
English writer/critic, 1984

[On Rock Hudson]

I feel sad for all of the thousands of women who fantasized about being in his arms, who now have to realize that he never really cared about them. I heard one older woman say, "I used to dream about him; too bad that he really didn't like erotic relations with women."

RUTH WESTHEIMER
American psychiatrist, 1984

The Gay closet has many points of discomfort. One is the sheer shame that life must be so secret, that one's citizenship is always dependent on how camouflaged as a heterosexual one appears. The necessary double life means that the Gay person can never simply stand flat-footed on the earth; there are always two people operating in one body, and one of them is a liar.

JUDITH GRAHN
American writer/activist, 1984

When I first came out, nothing scared me more than drag queens.

DARRELL YATES RIST
American writer/journalist, 1985

When your parents ask you why you're not married, don't say:
"Mom, Pop, there's something I have to tell you. I'm gay. I've always been gay and I just don't want to hide it anymore. I'm tired of living a lie. I hope you'll understand and that we can be a whole lot closer from now on. I'd like you to meet Sheldon."
Say:
"Married?! Are you nuts? With the stable of chicks *I've* built up? And I'm not talking dogs, I'm talking Class-A stuff. By the way, this is Shelly. He gets my leftovers, ha-ha."

TONY LANG
American humorist, 1985

"Coming out" is not an end point in the strategy of adjustment. Rather, it is a conceptual shortcut, an abbreviated way of thinking which fails to encompass the extremely complex process of managing discrediting information about oneself.

MARNY HALL
American psychotherapist/writer, 1986

When I was a youth, I thought that what is now known as "coming out" would alter society, but even then I did not expect that people in the public eye would make any declaration concerning their sex lives. That seemed too improbable.

Quentin Crisp
English writer/critic, 1986

Part of the James Dean legend had it that his younger costar [Sal Mineo] "turned queer" after Dean's untimely death in 1955. According to the story, Sal attempted fruitlessly to contact his fallen friend at a séance. He thereafter wrecked his car in an accident, but fate intervened to spare Sal's life. However, the words "James Dean" suddenly appeared on the car's windshield, and from that moment on, Sal Mineo was gay.

Boze Hadleigh
American writer, 1986

There's no need to remain in the closet in Provincetown. The energy that was previously used to build walls of self-protection can be used to create whatever kind of life you like.

Rondo Mieczkowski
American poet/writer, 1986

My evocation to gay people is to keep moving beyond the Myth of the Homosexual. Understand that being gay is not the same thing as being homosexual. A new wave in gay liberation is forming. In deep and profound ways, none of us has really "come out" yet.

Don Kilhefner
American writer/activist, 1987

"Coming out" is a deep occasion of the spirit that will not be swayed, of a mind that must know itself through the body. Then at last we're on our way; then we *make* our way.

AARON SHURIN
American writer, 1987

Coming out is more than a prescription to a contained lifestyle; it is an ongoing experience of many dimensions.

MARK THOMPSON
American writer, 1987

For me there's no closet to go back to. I don't have a thing to do with closets. I don't even see how you have the option to run back in once you run out and deal, and I prefer it out so much more.

ESSEX HEMPHILL
American poet, 1988

The truth popped out, and in popping out, the millstone was released, and I realized that being in the closet had been a terrible burden.

IAN MCKELLAN
English actor, 1988

There's a glorious, ecstatic feeling in being seen, in being out there, especially after so many years of hiding. This is me, come and take it.

SARA CYTRON
American comedian, 1988

What shall we say, who cringe and live,
  to those who fought and died,
and what excuses can we give?
  Where shall we hide?

QUENTIN CRISP
English writer/critic, 1988

I have no interest in educating my parents, my mother in particular.
While most of my friends are either out or waiting for their window
of opportunity, I'm keeping Momma from the truth.

JAMES MERRETT
American journalist, 1988

Whatever your sexuality is, there's nothing to be scared about. I
mean, there was a lot of fuss back in the time of Stonewall and gay
liberation about people "coming out." I was never in any kind of a
closet to come out of. It simply didn't occur to me to go into a closet.

DAVID STEVENS
Australian writer/director, 1988

Anglo gay boys are left much more to their own devices in coming-out
matters, but we've all had moments when something deep within us
revealed itself quite unexpectedly—if we knew how to look. Hidden
somewhere in the depths of my own closet is a childhood scrapbook
pasted with neatly colored drawings of the Empress Josephine and
England's Princess Margaret. Already at age 8, I was meditating on
crowns and robes and the meaning of the word *queen*.

HER IMPERIAL HIGHNESS
THE GRAND DUCHESS
TATIANA NEVAHOYDOVA
American socialite/journalist, 1988

Queers United Against Closets (or QUAC)

>American protest organization
>1988

No matter how far in or out of the closet you are—you have a next step.

>Ad slogan
>National March on Washington, 1988

EDUCATION

The notion that women need any education other than in good behavior and domestic science is hardly a hundred years old, and the word "coed" has been invented in my lifetime. For centuries, therefore, in a large part of the world, boys and adolescent young men have been educated in establishments where they met no girls for months on end. This period of their lives—from, say, nine to nineteen—took them well beyond the stage of mere sexual self-discovery, when masturbation was their only pastime, into their first attempts at erotic communication. This in the beginning takes the form of nothing more than a pooling of sexual energy. By their late teens, however, most Western men have begun to have elaborate and repeated fantasies and to select objects of desire in the real world. Naturally, at what in England are called public schools, these romantic longings focus on other boys or occasionally on the masters. In these circumstances it would be not unreasonable to suggest that the educational system is leading its victims into homosexuality.

Of course lasting harm could be done only to frail personalities—to borderline cases. Heterosexual men begin the pursuit of women immediately they leave school, while congenital homosexual men take to the brazen or covert quest of their own kind, but as Rupert Brooke said, "There are wanderers in the middle mist who know not if they love at all or, loving, whom." Such people are by no means always sex maniacs *who will try everything; sometimes they are timid idealists who do the least harm but incur the most opprobrium.*

When I was at school girls were naturally the subject of great interest, and the big question was whether or not you had seen "it." If you had, you had everyone on your side. Now, if you are really homosexual, you are never tempted by the possibility of heterosexual contact. At any time in my life I could sleep in the same bed with a girl. If she said, "I am cold," I would let her cuddle up with me, and I wouldn't have any sexual impulses at all. I did not ever have any genuine curiosity about the physical life of women. Coeducation was not likely to change a person like me.

When I was a child I never thought as a child. I subscribed meekly to my parents' idea that a good education was a protracted one. Scholarship seemed to them to be a weapon for use against a hostile world.

Education is in fact a last wild effort on the part of the authorities to prevent an overdose of leisure from driving the world mad, and learning is merely the most expensive time filler the world has ever known. Those who sink to the simple trading of facts insult their listeners. We can after all be offered only two kinds of information: what we already know, which is boring, and what we do not, which is humiliating.

By the very fact that we breathe our love into handsome boys we keep them from avarice, increase their enjoyment in work, trouble and dangers, and develop their modesty and self-control.

XENOPHON
Greek historian/essayist, 434 B.C.–355 B.C.

I am aware, sir, that Plato, in his Symposium, discourseth very eloquently touching the Uranian and Pandemian Venus: but you must remember that in our Universities, Plato is held to be little better than a misleader of youth.

THOMAS LOVE PEACOCK
English novelist/poet, 1785–1866
Dr. Folliott, in *Crotchet Castle*

At school, friendship is a passion. It entrances the being, it tears the soul. All loves of after-life can never bring its rapture, or its wretchedness; no bliss so absorbing, no pangs of jealousy or despair so crushing and so keen! What tenderness and what devotion; what illimitable confidence; infinite revelations of inmost thoughts; what ecstatic present and romantic future; what bitter estrangements and what melting reconciliations; what scenes of wild recrimination, agitating explanations, passionate correspondence; what insane sensitiveness, and what frantic sensibility; what earthquakes of the heart and whirlwinds of the soul are confined in that simple phrase, a schoolboy's friendship!

BENJAMIN DISRAELI
Prime Minister of Great Britain/author
1804–1881

The talk in the dormitories and studies was of the grossest character, with repulsive scenes of onanism, mutual masturbation and obscene orgies of naked boys in bed together.

[From his account of Harrow school for boys in England, 1852]

John Addington Symonds
English poet/essayist/literary historian
1840–1893

It is probable that the superior Urnings [gay people] will become, in affairs of the heart, to a large extent the teachers of the future society; and if that is so that their influence will tend to the realization and expression of an attachment less exclusively sensual than the average of today and to the diffusion of this in all directions.

Edward Carpenter
English writer/activist, 1844–1929

Oxford is the capital of Romance . . . in its own way as memorable as Athens and to me it was even more entrancing.

Oscar Wilde
Irish writer, 1854–1900

[Clive] educated Maurice, or rather his spirit educated Maurice's spirit, for they themselves became equal. Neither thought "Am I led; am I leading?" Love had caught him out of triviality and Maurice out of bewilderment in order that two imperfect souls might touch perfection.

E. M. Forster
English author, 1879–1970
Narrator, in *Maurice*

[From an interview two years after the closing of her play *The Drag*, a controversial portrait of homosexuals]

The theater will be my medium to sex education. I pride myself on the fact that I have always been ahead of public teachers. I realized the importance of the problem and devoted my career in the theater to the education of the masses. I shall boldly continue to do so, in spite of criticism, insults, and narrow-minded bigots. I believe that when I have my own theater, as I hope to some time in the future, my purpose can go unhindered by silly and old-fashioned taboos and busy bodies.

MAE WEST
American actress/playwright, 1892–1980

I hadn't been in prep school more than a month, and I'd slept with all the boys and half the faculty. . . . Of course, I'm speaking rhetorically!

TRUMAN CAPOTE
American writer, 1924–1984

"Wasn't it easy being a school-teacher?" I said. "Oh, it was," he said, "it was terrible. And the boys, you know, are such terrible tarts. Once one of them called me into the music room and we sat down and he kissed me, and I mean, what can one do? I didn't dare respond. So I simply smiled and pushed the boy off, with instruction to continue the five-finger exercise."

JOE ORTON
English playwright, 1933–1967

Did you hear about the transvestite at Harvard that wanted to spend his junior year abroad?

American joke, 1970s

We have no stake in education which is racist, male-chauvinist, anti-working class and antihomosexual. The schools are not people's schools and therefore do not serve the people. They certainly do not serve us as homosexuals, but teach ideology that is destructive to us and helps to keep us social outcasts. What child would have disdain for homosexuals? They have to be taught that.

CHICAGO GAY LIBERATION FOR
THE REVOLUTIONARY PEOPLE'S
CONSTITUTIONAL CONVENTION
Working Paper, 1970

I have often thought that a solution for the ills of the world would be to send all boys to a school that taught them to love one another. . . . I mean get them all into bed together to learn the ecstatic habit of male love.

JAMES BROUGHTON
American poet/playwright/filmmaker, 1982

By the persistent use of the term *homophile* (instead of the hetero designate gemixtepickle *homosexual*) we educated American public opinion to perceive us no longer as merely perverse performers of criminal acts but as *persons* of a distinct sociopolitical minority.

HARRY HAY
American writer/activist, 1987

[Quote embroidered on the Quilt panel commemorating his death from AIDS]

My anger is, that the government failed to educate us.

BILLY DENVER DONALD
American administrator for the
handicapped, 1987

[Comment regarding a Senate proposal permitting religious colleges in Washington, D.C., to deny facilities to gay student groups]

This amendment should go down into the sewer from whence it came.

LOWELL WEICKER
U.S. Senator (R. Conn.), 1988

In Utah, teachers are not allowed to talk about same-sex intercourse as a method of transmission. In Florida, state law requires that parents write permission notes before their children can be told about AIDS. And in countless other school districts around the country, controversial subject matter is simply ignored.

ROBERT W. PETERSON
American journalist/activist, 1988

All persons, regardless of sexual orientation, should be afforded equal opportunity within the public education system.

NATIONAL EDUCATION
ASSOCIATION
1988

I don't think it's my job to educate people on safe sex. Do I have to wear a condom in my scenes on the screen? This is an R-rated film. This is the '80s. There is AIDS. There is alcoholism. People should be able to figure it out for themselves.

TOM CRUISE
American actor, 1988

EMPLOYMENT AND MONEY

By homosexual men, though never by homosexual women, it is often claimed that, as a species, they exhibit greater artistic abilities than ordinary mortals. A long list of actors, sculptors, painters, writers is flaunted before the eyes of the world in an effort to present homosexuality in a favorable light. This well-meaning ploy hardly succeeds. Even the most ill-informed among us knows that, in general, artists, in whatever medium, have an evil reputation; they are drunkards and libertines and are known for neither fulfilling their contracts nor paying their debts.

It is also quite untrue to say that the preponderance of great artists is homosexual; they are merely the ones that cause the greatest scandal. What is true is that would-be employees, who would at a pinch accept any kind of work, if they cultivate a Bohemian appearance will get stuck with the arts however little talent they may, in fact, possess. Because real work is denied them—because banks will not employ them—they end up in photographic or advertising studios or backstage or in the lower depths of the movie industry. If they go so far as to look totally unacceptable, they attempt one or another of these professions but in a free-lance capacity. In other words, they return to being unemployed.

Recently, by appealing to the laws of the land, they have begun to try to force companies to employ them. Strange to relate, the law is on their side but, of course, real life is not. In practice, no statute on earth can for long compel any employer to use the services of somebody that, for whatever reason, he doesn't like. No boss will be foolish enough to say, "I don't want a bunch of faggots waltzing round my factory floor." He will bide his time until he can claim that the work of the undesirable employee is unsatisfactory.

When I was young I myself was forced into pseudo-artistic ways of earning a living. I never did anything well and am relieved now to be too old for any kind of employment whatsoever. I never liked work. Nay, I can say more. Before I do anything at all, I always ask myself one vital question: Can I possibly get out of this?

Many men . . . have spent a talent for a male lover or 300 drachmas
for a jar of caviar from the Black Sea.

> POLYBIUS
> Greek historian, 205? B.C.–125? B.C.

For all their faults and their annoying ways
With darling Ganymedes I'd pass my days,
Rather than lead a sumptuous tinselled life
With twenty million dollars and a wife.

> MARTIAL
> Roman poet/epigrammatist, 40–104

The fragrance of profit is pleasing; no one avoids gain.
Wealth, if I should speak plainly, does have a certain appeal.
Anyone who wishes to grow rich is willing to play this game:
If a man desires boys, he is willing to reward them.

> ANONYMOUS
> Medieval poet, 1120?
> From "Ganymede and Helen"

Though a lord may promise much,
And abject poverty constrain me . . .
I am not one of those inclined to do
What is profitable rather than proper. . . .
I prefer to remain poor and pure
Than to live wealthy and debauched.

> ANONYMOUS
> Medieval monk, 1200?
> From the "Carmina Burana"

JUPITER: Come, gentle Ganymede, and play with me:
   I love thee well, say Juno what she will. . . .
GANYMEDE: I would have a jewel for mine ear,
   And a fine brooch to put in my hat,
   And then I'll hug with you an hundred times.

> CHRISTOPHER MARLOWE
> English poet/playwright, 1564–1593
> From "Dido, Queen of Carthage"

There now ye sit, and with mixt souls embrace,
Gazing upon great *Love's* mysterious Face,
And pity this base world where *Friendship's* made
A bait for sin, or else at best a *Trade*.

> ABRAHAM COWLEY
> English poet, 1618–1667
> From "David and Jonathan"

This practice [homosexuality] took away not only our own living, but
something from all womankind which nature intended them to have.

> JOHN CLELAND
> English novelist, 1709–1789
> Fanny Hill, in *Memoirs of Fanny Hill*

THE CUPBEARER SPEAKS

Prithee leave me, crafty hussy,
  Take thy ringlets brown away:
To my master suits my waiting
  And his kisses are my pay.
Therefore thou, I'm free to wager,
  Hast no love on me to spend:
And thy cheeks, thy breasts, would only
  Be fatiguing to my friend.

> Johann Wolfgang von Goethe
> German poet, 1749–1832

Everywhere a new motive of life dawns.
With the liberation of Love, and with it of Sex, with the sense
that these are things—and the joy of them—not to be dreaded or
barred, but to be made use of, wisely and freely, as a man makes
use of his most honored possession,
Comes a new gladness:
The liberation of a Motive greater than Money,
And the only motive perhaps that can finally take precedence of
Money.

> Edward Carpenter
> English writer/activist, 1844–1929
> From "A Mightier than Mammon"

One could never pay too high a price for any sensation.

> Oscar Wilde
> Irish writer, 1854–1900

I felt that this was the man who wanted money from me. I said, "I suppose you have come about my beautiful letter to Lord Alfred Douglas." . . . He said, "A man offered me £60 for it." I said to him, "If you take my advice you will go to that man and sell my letter to him for £60. I myself have never received so large a sum for any prose work of that length; but I am glad to find that there is someone in England who considers a letter of mine worth £60."

[His description to the prosecutor at his first trial for homosexual acts regarding his conference with a blackmailer]

OSCAR WILDE
Irish writer, 1854–1900

No man is rich enough to buy back his past.

OSCAR WILDE
Irish writer, 1854–1900

C. F. GILL, prosecutor at Wilde's second trial: You made handsome presents to all these young fellows?

OSCAR WILDE: Pardon me, I differ. I gave two or three of them a cigarette case. Boys of that class smoke a good deal of cigarettes. I have a weakness for presenting my acquaintances with cigarette cases.

GILL: Rather an expensive habit if indulged in indiscriminately, isn't it?

WILDE: Less extravagant than giving jewelled garters to ladies.

OSCAR WILDE
Irish writer, 1854–1900

The bringing up of boys by male persons (slaves in the ancient times) seems to favor homosexuality; the frequency of inversion in the present-day nobility is probably explained by their employment of male servants, and by the scant care that mothers of that class give to their children.

Sigmund Freud
Austrian neurologist/founder of
psychoanalysis, 1856–1939

Many of our famous lawyers, doctors, bankers and judges are homosexualists. Thousands of others suffer because they are starving for love both in body and soul, and they become mental prostitutes.

Mae West
American actress/playwright, 1892–1980

I have some lady impersonators in the play [*Pleasure Man*]. In fact, I have five of them. But what of it? If they are going to close up the play and prevent these people from making a living because they take the part of female impersonators, then they should stop other female impersonators from appearing on the Keith Circuit. . . . How many thousand female impersonators do you think there are in the country? Are they going to put them all out of business?

Mae West
American actress/playwright, 1892–1980

The instinct of acquisitiveness has more perverts, I believe, than the instinct of sex. . . . People seem to me odder about money than about even their amours. Such amazing meannesses as one's always coming across, particularly among the rich.

Aldous Huxley
English novelist/critic, 1894–1963

It was very much easier for us because we were in the arts. We were never employed by anybody who demanded any kind of concealment, and we were largely on our own—not pleasing any boss, as it were, except ourselves, and that made it easier.

CHRISTOPHER ISHERWOOD
English writer, 1904–1986

Just being gay really keeps you busy from morn until eve if you do it whole-heartedly . . . if you're constantly working for your gay brothers and sisters.

CHRISTOPHER ISHERWOOD
English writer, 1904–1986

The sexual friendship of two young men, or young girls, follows the lines of economic cleavage when marriage is too expensive or the penalty of illicit intercourse too dear.

T. H. EVANS
American sexologist/psychiatrist, 1906

I was not attracted sexually to the old men whom I robbed; what attracted me was their money; so the question was to take their money by beating them or by making them come; the goal was money.

JEAN GENET
French playwright/writer, 1910–1986

[Comment regarding his rejection from the draft]

I've been turned down for everything, including the WACs.

TRUMAN CAPOTE
American writer, 1924–1984

[Motto encouraging gay patronage of gay businesses, inspired by Harvey Milk's slogan "Gay for Gay"]

Gay Buy Gay.

> HARVEY MILK
> American politician/activist, 1930–1978

A large bank balance in a gathering of queers is as popular as a large prick.

> JOE ORTON
> English playwright, 1933–1967

To be young, good-looking, healthy, famous, comparatively rich and happy is surely going against nature, and when to the above list one adds that daily I have the company of beautiful fifteen-year-old boys who find (for a small fee) fucking with me a delightful sensation, no man can want for more.

> JOE ORTON
> English playwright, 1933–1967

I often get picked up by queers 'round here. Some of them have very nice places. They must be on quite good money. I've had as much as thirty shillings from some of them.

> JOE ORTON
> English playwright, 1933–1967
> Spoken by a fellow Orton picked up once

Hustled? *Me?* No. I never charged no one in my life—and I could have, too. But I tell you this: Some of my relatives, over in Sicily, are *ragazzi di vita.*

> SAL MINEO
> American actor, 1939–1976

Transsexuals who continue to work in the same field after surgery often must sacrifice the status and salary they have earned, reentering the field on a lower level than formerly, under a new name.

> HARRIET SLAVITZ
> American sexologist, 1960s

Inverts [homosexuals] are to be found in every conceivable line of work from truck driving to coupon clipping. But they are most concentrated—or most noticeable—in the fields of the creative and performing arts and industries serving women's beauty and fashion needs.

> *The New York Times*, 1963

Homosexuals as well as heterosexuals have emotional hangups. Though that usually comes to an abrupt end—when the boy asks for more money.

> GORE VIDAL
> American writer, 1969

The jobs into which we are tracked are often low-paying and certainly alienating. And the higher federal income taxation of "single" people—that is, those whose relationships are not recognized as legal—discriminates against us economically.

Chicago Gay Liberation for
the Revolutionary People's
Constitutional Convention
Working Paper, 1970

[Truman Capote] thinks he's a very rich Society Lady, and spends a great deal of money.

Gore Vidal
American writer, 1973

There is a manneristic fairydom that depends on money, chic, privilege and exclusive, monopolistic high style, and I would say that it is usually accompanied by bitchiness and bad manners and faithless love, too. I like homosexuality where the lovers are friends all their lives, and there are many lovers and many friends.

Allen Ginsberg
American poet, 1975

You have to polish up your raw identity until it becomes a lifestyle: something interesting by which you are proud to be identified, and something with which you can do barter with the outer world to get from it what you want.

Quentin Crisp
English writer/critic, 1979

Never try to keep up with the Joneses—drag them down to your level.
It's cheaper.

> QUENTIN CRISP
> English writer/critic, 1979

You can convert your style into riches.

> QUENTIN CRISP
> English writer/critic, 1979

It's no good running a pig farm badly for thirty years while saying,
"Really I was meant to be a ballet dancer." By that time, pigs will
be your style.

> QUENTIN CRISP
> English writer/critic, 1979

If I am rich, it is because I have taken my wages in people. You are
my reward.

> QUENTIN CRISP
> English writer/critic, 1979

Some of you may be so old-fashioned that you still have jobs. If this
is so, try not to get stuck in work where you only deal with things—
and I include the highest possible level of things. Sculpture, books,
paintings—they are only objects—just like washing machines, but
not so useful.

> QUENTIN CRISP
> English writer/critic, 1979

I have some good news and some bad news. I just found out my
    son is a homosexual.
What's the good news?
He's dating a doctor.

American joke, 1980s

Yes, you know *gay*,
but I need to teach you *queer*
I need to tell you about hostile glares
and false arrests
and you have no defense
a queer can't bear witness
against a lying cop. They call your boss,
you lose your job, there's no redress.

MARTHA SHELLEY
American activist/poet, 1982

As for jeans, cowboy shirts and work boots, they at least have the
virtue of being cheap. The uniform conceals the rise of what strikes
me as a whole new class of gay indigents. Sometimes I have the
impression every fourth man on Christopher Street is out of work,
but the poverty is hidden by the costume. Whether this appalling
situation should be disguised is another question altogether; is it
somehow egalitarian to have both the rich and the poor dressed up
as Paul Bunyan?

EDMUND WHITE
American novelist/essayist, 1983

Heterosexuals are not presumed to be sexually irresponsible when they are interviewed for a job, nor are they required to promise chastity. Why should homosexuals be discriminated against in this regard when they seek employment? . . . If it be such a criterion, it should apply to heterosexual as well as homosexual people. . . . I urge him [Mayor Koch] to stand strong against the use of public funds in agencies where equal rights are denied.

PAUL MOORE, JR.
Episcopal Bishop of New York, 1984
From his letter to *The New York Times*

Many of my friends were able to find work in camouflage. This seemed an unlikely way for me to earn a living. My function in life was to render clear what was already blindingly conspicuous.

QUENTIN CRISP
English writer/critic, 1984

What better proof of love can there be than money? A ten-shilling note showed incontrovertibly just how mad about you a man is. Even in the minds of some women a confusion exists between love and money if the quantity is large enough.

QUENTIN CRISP
English writer/critic, 1984

Ironically, the work situation itself often contributes to a compulsive working style in gay men. This is so because it is often necessary to conceal one's homosexuality to varying degrees at work, and to lead a double life with varying degrees of deception and avoidance. Even when coworkers are tolerant or accepting, a company may worry about its image and customer attitudes. Insecurity intensifies when one is passed over for promotion. Self-doubt raises anxiety, compelling the individual to work harder.

RONALD E. HELLMAN
American psychiatrist, 1985

Don't go to piano bars where young, unemployed actors get up and sing. Definitely don't *be* a young, unemployed actor who gets up and sings.

TONY LANG
American humorist, 1985

It is suddenly all right to be a hairdresser. No one really knows how this happened.

TONY LANG
American humorist, 1985

Large corporations have never been particularly congenial settings for workers who have diverged from the norms of white, heterosexual, male society. A lesbian who works in such a setting has to face two levels of devaluation: her femaleness and her lesbianism. If she is not white and Anglo-Saxon, she adds a third.

MARNY HALL
American psychotherapist/writer, 1986

[Comment regarding the corporation's written ban on discrimination against gay people]

We value differences at Apple. As we prepare for the future, we must remember that diversity in the workplace adds richness.

DEBBIE BIONDOLILLO
American personnel director
Apple Computer, Inc.

AZT. Whatever you may think of its use as a drug, it was the first ever to be denied to people on the basis of cost factor alone.

SIMON WATNEY
American linguist/writer, 1988

[Regarding her legal dispute with the U.S. Army Reserve to reenlist her after she was discharged for being gay (she won)]

I will not live with a discharge that says I'm honorable but unfit to serve my country.

MIRIAM BEN-SHALOM
American soldier, 1988

[Regarding the people commemorated on the Quilt]

There are policemen, schoolteachers, farmers, doctors, playwrights, ministers, chefs, lawyers, artists and politicians. There is a quilt panel for the hairdresser who styled Joan Mondale's hair during the 1984 Democratic Convention, and there is one for the respiratory therapist who tended Ronald Reagan after the 1981 assassination attempt. There are sons and daughters, mothers and fathers, lovers, brothers, friends and grandparents.

CINDY RUSKIN
American activist, 1988

Someone once suggested that we start a gay bank. My immediate reaction was: For heaven's sake, let's let money be sexless.

QUENTIN CRISP
English writer/critic, 1988

GAYNESS

I have no idea when the modern meaning of the word "gay" first emerged into general consciousness. I was still only English when shortly after the Second World War, it arrived in Britain. I think its use was intended to mark the blossoming of a new self-esteem in homosexual men and women.

There have been almost as many words invented to designate a homosexual man as there are for the sexual organs. Presumably the word "homosexual" was thought to be too long and too clinical for conversational use but the word "queer" was too derogatory for the up-market view of themselves that homosexuals were starting to hold. The words "fairy" and "pansy" were also losing favor but for different reasons— among them, that they did not take into account females of homosexual persuasion.

The gay scene inevitably parodies real life. There was once a more marked difference between the sexes. Among homosexual men and women alike there was also a positive and a negative pole. In each relationship, however brief or haphazard, there was a masculine and a feminine party, a pursuer and a pursued. In those days the passive member in a courtship accepted epithets denoting his or her femininity willingly—even eagerly.

Now the notion of a wooing—of anybody being hard to get—has disappeared from the face of the earth. Women are prepared to frequent singles bars, which, after all, are nothing more than brothels—worse than brothels because the justification that money will be earned is lacking. The same hideous crudity prevails in the homosexual world. The word "gay" because it is short and breezy seems at first appropriate but really it is ironic.

As the Hungarian humorist Mr. Mikes has pointed out, gay is precisely what the homosexual community is not. In fact, a significant section of it has become grim—forever demanding its rights and shaking its fist in the face of the establishment.

To me the disadvantage of the new use of the word "gay" is not its inappropriateness but the fact that it has been the death of good lyric writing. The divine Nan Wynn used to sing a song that began "Till today I was gay." Who would dare to utter such a statement in public today?

Whatever gayness itself is I do not know. It's apparent that it varies from individual to individual. I myself never wandered in the middle mist. From the dawn of history I was effeminate. I did not want to play games, I did not want to get hurt, I did not even want to go out in the world. I wanted to stay home. I felt at home with girls and women. I understood (or thought I understood) their province. From about the age of sixteen on I spent my life with women who told me about their broken hearts. I never questioned that. That's what I found myself doing. And from the age of four or five I was waltzing round the house in clothes that I'd found in an attic that belonged to my mother or my grandmother, saying, "I will be a beautiful princess and you will kneel."

Fifty years ago, when many more people than today believed that effeminacy was synonymous with homosexuality, I mistakenly presumed that I represented homosexuality by being effeminate. Now I know that I represent nothing grander than my puny self. In recent years, as I have made many more friends among heterosexuals and been subject to attacks by gay people, this awareness—that I am first and last an individual, not a spokesman for any group—has been made all the more clear to me.

When the very center of your being—in my case my ambiguous

gender—becomes a subject of scorn, there isn't much choice about how to respond to the world: either you say, "I'm awfully sorry, I see how wrong it is, I will not be homosexual from now onward," or else you have to say, "I cannot be otherwise, this is the way I am. If you can't bear it, then we must never meet again."

There is now in England a law (commonly called "Section 28") that makes it illegal to do, say, or write anything that promotes the idea of a homosexual lifestyle. This statute and anybody unfortunate enough to be caught in its web are likely to be in for a lot of argument. It is not going to be easy to define its exact meaning, but if it is an attempt to prevent anyone from suggesting that gay is the same as happy, I would expect most people to be in the clear. Who in his right mind would recommend a way of life that leads to perpetual physical danger and is, often, so sterile and so lonely?

Homosexual urges are primitive and far too deeply rooted for legislation to reach them, though homosexual practices can, in timid people, be curbed.

The only thing that can be taught is that recommending a normal way of life to a confirmed homosexual person is as hopeless an undertaking as the reverse.

The difference between public attitudes toward homosexuality in the 1920s and today is that nowadays people generally take offense only to things that are genuinely offensive. In earlier times people took offense to everything that fell outside their petty tolerances. Today most people seem to realize that "who sleeps with whom" is just about the least of society's problems.

Blest is the man who loves and after early play
   Whereby his limbs are supple made and strong,
   Retiring to his house, with wine and song
Toys with a fair boy on his breast the livelong day!

> SOLON
> Athenian statesman, 638? B.C.–558? B.C.

Golden-haired love strikes me again
with a purple ball, and calls on me to play
with a motley-sandled girl. But she,
for she comes from well-built Lesbos,
finds fault with my hair, for it is white,
and gapes after another girl.

> ANACREON
> Greek poet, 572? B.C.–488? B.C.

Those who love men and rejoice to lie with and be embraced by men
are also the finest boys and young men, being naturally the most
manly. The people who accuse them of shamelessness lie; they do this
not from shamelessness but from courage, manliness, and virility,
embracing what is like them. A clear proof of this is the fact that as
adults they alone acquit themselves as men in public careers.

> ARISTOPHANES
> Athenian playwright, 450? B.C.–385? B.C.

Give me a boy whose tender skin
Owes its fresh bloom to youth, not art;
And for his sake may no girl win
A place in my heart.

> MARTIAL
> Roman poet/epigrammatist, 40–104

Indeed . . . there is some danger that womankind will become unnecessary in the future, with young men instead fulfilling all the needs women used to.

> ST. JOHN CHRYSOSTOM
> Bishop of Constantinople, 347–407

What can there be of as much value as a boy faithful to his lover?

> MARBOD
> French Bishop of Rennes, 1060?–1123

While I was still a schoolboy, the charm of my friends greatly captivated me, so that among the foibles and failings with which that age is fraught, my mind surrendered itself completely to emotion and devoted itself to love.

> ST. AELRED OF RIEVAULX
> English historical writer/abbot, 1109?–1166

"Disparity divides things: it is rather like things that are rightly
    joined together;
For a man to be linked to a man is a more elegant coupling.
In case you had not noticed, there are certain rules of grammar
By which articles of the same gender must be coupled together."

> ANONYMOUS
> Medieval poet, 1120?
> Ganymede, in the poem "Ganymede and
> Helen"

Many the girls and women I have loved, both lad and man; many the boys and men I have loved, both lad and man.

> ANONYMOUS
> German monk, 1150?

Many you will find for whom the boyish sin is execrable in words
But who do not dislike the deed.
The more they detest it with their words—to hide what they love
    and freely do—
The more they indulge it in their acts.

> ANONYMOUS
> Medieval monk, 1150?

The indiscriminate Venus grasps at any remedy,
But the wise one rejoices with the tender Ganymede.

I have heard it said that he plays Venus more than she,
But Venus is happy, since he only does boys.

Nothing is more certain than this, that Venus would
Be devoid of every sweetness if she lacked Ganymede.

For his face smiles, his complexion shines, his legs are soft,
His lap is sweet, his heart gentle and his beauty charming;
His demeanor is open, suppressing shyness, his spirit
Is ready for the boyish sin, and his body prepared
To undergo anything his seducer should ask:
This boy surpasses all treasure; nothing is more blessed than he.

> ANONYMOUS
> Medieval monk, 1150?

The love of which I speak aspires on high;
Woman is too unlike and little does it agree
With a wise and manly heart to burn for her.
The one draws up to heaven, the other down to earth,
The one inhabits the soul, the other the senses.

> MICHELANGELO BUONARROTI
> Italian sculptor/painter/architect/poet
> 1475–1564

All they that love not tobacco and boys are fools.

CHRISTOPHER MARLOWE
English poet/playwright, 1564–1593

Great Alexander loved Hephaestion,
The conquering Hercules for Hylas wept,
And for Patroclus stern Achilles drooped.
And not kings only, but the wisest men:
The Roman Tully loved Octavius,
Grave Socrates, wild Alcibiades.

CHRISTOPHER MARLOWE
English poet/playwright, 1564–1593

Two loves I have of comfort and despair
    Which like two spirits do suggest me still,
The better angel is a man right fair,
    The worser spirit a woman colored ill.

WILLIAM SHAKESPEARE
English playwright/poet, 1564–1616

Farewell, woman! I intend
    Henceforth every night to sit
With my lewd, well-natured friend,
    Drinking to engender wit.

Then give me health, wealth, mirth, and wine,
    And, if busy love entrenches,
There's a sweet, soft page of mine
    Does the trick worth forty wenches.

JOHN WILMOT,
EARL OF ROCHESTER
English poet, 1648–1680

Englishmen were dolts and nidwits not to realize that there was better sport than with women.

> ROBERT HARLEY,
> EARL OF OXFORD
> English statesman, 1661–1724

How did it come about that a vice which would destroy mankind if it were general, that a sordid outrage against nature, is still so natural?

> VOLTAIRE
> French philosopher/scientist/writer
> 1694–1778

Women are kept for nothing but the breed;
For pleasure we must have a Ganymede,
A fine, fresh Hylas, a delicious boy,
To serve our purposes of beastly joy.

> CHARLES CHURCHILL
> English poet/satirist, 1731–1764

The Greeks knew the difference between love and friendship as well as we—they had distinct terms to signify them by: it seems reasonable therefore to suppose that when they say love they mean love, and that when they say friendship only they mean friendship only.

> JEREMY BENTHAM
> English jurist/philosopher, 1748–1832

We two boys together clinging,
One the other never leaving,
Up and down the roads going, North and South excursions making,
Power enjoying, elbows stretching, fingers clutching,
Arm'd and fearless, eating, drinking, sleeping, loving,
No law less than ourselves owning, sailing, soldiering, thieving,
    threatening,
Misers, menials, priests alarming, air breathing, water drinking, on
    the turf or the sea-beach dancing,
Cities wrenching, ease scorning, statutes mocking, feebleness chas-
    ing,
Fulfilling our foray.

WALT WHITMAN
American poet, 1819–1892

The prairie-grass dividing, its special odor breathing, I demand of it
the spiritual corresponding, Demand the most copious and close
companionship of men.

WALT WHITMAN
American poet, 1819–1892

I will make the most splendid race the sun ever shone upon, I will
make divine magnetic lands. . . . I will make inseparable cities with
their arms about each other's necks, by the love of comrades.

WALT WHITMAN
American poet, 1819–1892

Pederasty is a disease with which all men are stricken at a certain
age.

GUSTAVE FLAUBERT
French novelist, 1821–1880

EDWARD CARSON, prosecutor at Wilde's trial: What enjoyment was it to you to entertain grooms and coachmen?

OSCAR WILDE: The pleasure to me was being with those who are young, bright, happy, careless, and free. I do not like the sensible and I do not like the old.

> OSCAR WILDE
> Irish writer, 1854–1900
> From the transcript of his first trial

I would sooner have fifty unnatural vices than one unnatural virtue.

> OSCAR WILDE
> Irish writer, 1854–1900

The natural attraction between young men & young women is pretty sure to be stronger than this unnatural & fantastic one between girl & girl; but it [the former] can't go to such lengths among respectable young people.

> ALICE STONE BLACKWELL
> American feminist, 1882

All men are capable of homosexual object selection and actually accomplish this in the unconscious.

> SIGMUND FREUD
> Austrian neurologist/founder of
> psychoanalysis, 1856–1939

Some of the most prominent men known have been inverts [homosexuals] and perhaps absolute inverts.

SIGMUND FREUD
Austrian neurologist/founder of
psychoanalysis, 1856–1939

I tried to persuade myself that I was three-quarters normal and that only a quarter of me was queer—whereas really it was the other way round.

SOMERSET MAUGHAM
English novelist/playwright, 1874–1965

Went out last night,
With a crowd of my friends,
They must be womens
Cause I don't like mens.

MA RAINEY
American singer, 1886–1939

The anomaly [gay love] has been in existence as long as man has. It has been called by many names, some opprobrious, some laudatory. Now that the world dares say sex and sexuality aloud, it seems to be agreed that such individuals shall be called homosexuals, though they, if one may judge from their writings on the subject, prefer to be called "the intermediate sex."

JOSEPH COLLINS
American neurologist, 1866–1950

Genuine homosexuality is not a vice, it is an endowment.

JOSEPH COLLINS
American neurologist, 1866–1950

Maids, not to you my mind doth change;
Men I defy, allure, estrange,
Prostrate, make bond or free:
Soft as the stream beneath the plane
To you I sing my love's refrain;
Between us is no thought of pain,
   Peril, satiety.

> EDITH EMMA COOPER (1862–1914)
> AND KATHERINE HARRIS BRADLEY
> (1846–1914)
> English poets/playwrights
> From "Variations on Sappho"

I find pleasure in watching women in each other's arms, waltzing well.

> GABRIELLE SIDONIE COLETTE
> French novelist, 1873–1954

She [the character Helen Furr] told many then the way of being gay, she taught very many then little ways they could use in being gay. She was living very well, she was gay then, she went on living then, she was regular in being gay, she always was living very well and was gay very well and was telling about little ways one could be learning to use in being gay, and later was telling them quite often, telling them again and again.

> GERTRUDE STEIN
> American writer, 1874–1946
> From *Miss Furr and Miss Skeene*

Happiest of all, surely, are those Uranians, ever numerous, who have no wish nor need to fly society—or themselves. Knowing what they are, understanding the natural, moral strength of their position as homosexuals; sure of right on their side, even if it be never accorded to them in the lands where they must live; fortunate in either due self-control or private freedom—day by day, they go through their lives, self-respecting and respected, in relative peace.

EDWARD STEVENSON
(Born Xavier Mayne)
American sexologist, 1908

I don't know what I am; no one's ever told me that I'm different and yet I know that I'm different—that's why, I suppose, you've felt as you have done. And for that I forgive you, though whatever it is, it was you and my father who made this body—but what I will never forgive is your daring to try and make me ashamed of my love. I'm not ashamed of it, there's no shame in me.

RADCLYFFE HALL
English novelist, 1886–1943
Stephen Gordon, in *The Well of Loneliness*

Lesbian love as the designation of love relationships between women is widely used and its meaning is universally understood, at least by all persons at all versed in sexual science. Yet the standard dictionaries which list medical terms . . . take no notice of the terms relating to sexual inversion in women.

DOUGLAS C. MCMURTRIE
American psychologist/sexologist
1888–1944

Chicago has not developed a euphemism yet for these male perverts. In New York they are known as "fairies" and wear a red necktie (inverts are generally said to prefer green). In Philadelphia they are known as "Brownies."

> JAMES G. KIERNAN
> American sexologist, 1916

Homosexuality then is love for members of the same sex. It begins at home among brothers and brothers, sisters and sisters, and has always united mothers and daughters, fathers and sons, in bonds of friendly love.

> CONSTANCE LONG
> American physician/sexologist, 1919

Many people fail to recognize homosexuality when they see it.

> LA FOREST POTTER
> American psychoanalyst, 1933

[Admiring the view from Somerset Maugham's villa in the Mediterranean, known as a gathering place for distinguished gay artists of the day]

Oh, Mr. Maugham, but this is a fairyland!

> EDNA ST. VINCENT MILLAY
> American writer, 1892–1950

Come all ye Revelers!—Dance the night unto dawn—come when you like, with whom you like—wear what you like— Unconventional? Oh, to be sure—only do be discreet!

> Poster advertising gay dance
> The Greenwich Village Ball, 1930

When you see two women walking hand in hand,
  Just look 'em over and try to understand:
They'll go to those parties—have the lights down low—
  Only those parties where women can go.

> BESSIE SMITH
> American singer, 1894–1937
> From "The Boy in the Boat"

Ten percent of all men are more or less exclusively homosexual for at least three years between the ages of 16 and 55.

> ALFRED KINSEY
> American zoologist/sociologist/sexologist
> 1894–1956

Listen. You're a hell of a good guy, and I'm fonder of you than anybody on earth. I couldn't tell you that in New York. It'd mean I was a faggot.

> ERNEST HEMINGWAY
> American novelist, 1899–1961
> Bill Gorton, in *The Sun Also Rises*

Ah, yes, that word [*gay*]. Well, it belonged to another time. Even if it didn't have the homosexual connotation, it would hardly be an adjective in popular usage nowadays. It's rather quaint. Perhaps a word like "homoerotic"—but they always object to the prefix "homo," except in Homo sapiens, and if it isn't one group that's objecting, it's another.

> GEORGE CUKOR
> American film director, 1899–1983

Isn't it curious that female homosexuals want a separate word for themselves, but there are no separate adjectives or nouns for female and male heterosexuals?

> GEORGE CUKOR
> American film director, 1899–1983

We stand in the middle of an uncharted, uninhabited country. That there have been other unions like ours is obvious, but we are unable to draw on their experience. We must create everything for ourselves. And creation is never easy.

[From a letter to his lover, Russell Cheney, British painter]

> FRANCIS OTTO MATTHIESSEN
> English writer/educator, 1902–1950

Homosexuality is more acceptable, only because blatant heterosexuality is more acceptable.

> CECIL BEATON
> British photographer/writer/film designer
> 1902–1980

I don't feel personally that I'm constantly a part of the gay community; rather a large majority of the people who come to this house happen to be gay.

> CHRISTOPHER ISHERWOOD
> English writer, 1904–1986

I couldn't possibly turn heterosexual; that would be like cowardice in the face of the enemy . . . or something you could never live down. I'd have to go live on one of the remote islands of the South Pacific, it would be such a disgrace.

CHRISTOPHER ISHERWOOD
English writer, 1904–1986

One is not born homosexual or normal; each person becomes one or the other according to the accidents in his life and his own reaction to these accidents.

JEAN-PAUL SARTRE
French philosopher/novelist/dramatist/critic
1905–1980

It is not only a man who can be dangerous to a woman. . . . In some cases it can be another woman.

EDOUARD BOURDET
French playwright, 1926
D'Aiguines, in *The Captive*

I don't have any theory about homosexuality. I don't even have a theory about undifferentiated desire. I ascertain that I'm homosexual. OK. That's no cause for alarm. How and why are idle questions.

JEAN GENET
French playwright/writer, 1910–1986

Man alone satisfies man.

JEAN GENET
French playwright/writer, 1910–1986

He was a boy, just a boy, when I was a very young girl. When I was sixteen, I made the discovery—love. All at once and much, much too completely. It was like you suddenly turned a blinding light on something that had always been half in shadow, that's how it struck the world for me. But I was unlucky. Deluded. There was something different about the boy, a nervousness, a softness and tenderness which wasn't like a man's, although he wasn't the least bit effeminate looking—still—that thing was there.

> TENNESSEE WILLIAMS
> American playwright, 1912–1983
> Blanche Dubois, in *A Streetcar Named Desire*

The time has come, I think, when we must recognize bisexuality as a normal form of human behavior.

> MARGARET MEAD
> American anthropologist, 1901–1978

We're saying this whole marvelous thing of being gay, of being a fairy, is much more than just the beautiful part of our sexuality. There is more to be explored and discovered. We're calling on gay people to come out and fly. This is what we think the movement of the age is.

> HARRY HAY
> American activist, 1950

It is not uncommon for lesbians to establish friendly relations with male homosexuals. One reason is that the relationship is apt to be a platonic one and consequently they have no need to fear being seduced, particularly if they harbor antipathy toward men in general.

> FRANK CAPRIO
> American sexologist, 1954

We have to not only affirm ourselves as an identity, but as a creative force.

> MICHEL FOUCAULT
> French author/philosopher, 1926–1984

My mother made me a homosexual.

If I gave her some yarn, would she make me one too?

> American graffito, 1960s

The very idea of changing to heterosexuality . . . is a tacit acknowledgment of inferiority.

> FRANK KAMENY
> American activist/founder of Washington
> Mattachine Society, 1965

[Horatio] Alger appeared to be living a kind of existence which was homosexual in nature, if not in fact. He had renounced women and the conventional patterns of sex. As far as anyone knows, he had no women friends. All his time was spent either with [Charles] O'Connor [superintendent of the Children's Aid Society Lodging House] or the young boys who surrounded them.

> JOHN TEBBEL
> American biographer, 1965

A woman lover is always persistent.

> HEDY LAMARR
> Actress, 1966

All over the United States there are young gay people who think they're going to fail *because* they're gay. I want to show them they can succeed—that they can have hope.

> HARVEY MILK
> American politician/activist, 1930–1978

I never was able to imagine myself as ordinary.

> JOE ORTON
> English playwright, 1933–1967

Our tragedy does not derive from our fantasy of what homosexuals are but from our fantasy of what America is. We have made each other up.

> ELDRIDGE CLEAVER
> American black activist/writer, 1968
> Beverly Axelrod, in *Soul on Ice*

Homosexuals have time for everybody . . . every detail of lives of real people, however mundane it may be, seems romantic to them.

> QUENTIN CRISP
> English writer/critic, 1968

I am going to use the slang term "gay" as a synonym for homosexual, though I by no means wish to imply by this use that homosexual life is gay in the more traditional sense of the word.

> MARTIN HOFFMAN
> American psychologist/sexologist, 1968

Society deals with homosexuality as if it did not exist.

> MARTIN HOFFMAN
> American psychologist/sexologist, 1968

There once was a gay chap named Bloom,
Who invited a gent to his room.
They argued all night
As to who had the right
To do what with which and to whom.

> English limerick, 1970s

Did you hear about the young man who moved to Greenwich Village and turned prematurely gay?

> American joke, 1970s

Gay is a process of attaining mutual and equal social and sensual relationships among all human beings, which is realized only through participation in the free dynamic expression of love among people of the same sex.

> GAY REVOLUTION PARTY
> Manifesto, 1970

[Title of their book about lesbianism and society]

Sappho Was a Right-On Woman

> SIDNEY ABBOTT AND
> BARBARA LOVE
> American writers, 1972

Fag, faggot, dyke, queer, lezzie, homo, fairy, mary, pansy, sissy, etc., are terms of abuse. If you don't want to insult, the words are gay, lesbian and homosexual.

Gay Activists Alliance and
National Gay Task Force
1973

I prefer the word faggot which I tend to use myself. I have never allowed actively in my life the word "gay" to pass my lips. I don't know why I hate that word.

Gore Vidal
American writer, 1973

[Truman Capote] falls in love passionately with air-conditioning repair men. He had a tragic affair recently with an air-conditioning repair man.

Gore Vidal
American writer, 1973

There is that lovely story about Tennessee Williams. When he was making a movie, there was a young man around at a party. One of the directors came up and said, "What do you do?" And he said, "I sleep with Mr. Williams," which is a position in itself.

Lou Harrison
American composer, 1974

With communication overt, homosexual lovemaking is obviously terrific and charming. Without communication it's a drag, and heterosexuals the same.

Allen Ginsberg
American poet, 1975

Gay is too much of a category!

> ALLEN GINSBERG
> American poet, 1975

The answer to the question "Who is a homosexual?" depends somewhat on who is asking and who is choosing to say.

> C. A. TRIPP
> American writer/sexologist, 1975

You know, I made it with Kerouac quite often.

> ALLEN GINSBERG
> American poet, 1975

I wonder if Socrates and Plato took a house on Crete during the summer.

> WOODY ALLEN
> American screenwriter/director/actor, 1975
> From *Love and Death*

I got a girl in every port and a couple of guys in every port, too.

> SAL MINEO
> American actor, 1939–1976

As long as you don't wear a dress or sound like Marilyn Monroe, there's no problem that can't be worked out. One time, when my Ma wondered how come I turned out gay, I asked her, "Ma, how come my brothers *didn't?*"

> SAL MINEO
> American actor, 1939–1976

Since I don't recognize such a thing as a heterosexual personality, how can I define or detect a homosexual personality?

> Gore Vidal
> American writer, 1977

Aside from the production of children, homosexuals alone can fulfill satisfactorily human needs, wants, and desires, all the while supporting and sustaining a human community remarkable by the very fact that it is unremarkable.

> B. R. Burg
> American historian/writer, 1977

The male engaging in sexual activity aboard a pirate ship in the West Indies three centuries past was simply an ordinary member of his community, completely socialized and acculturated.

> B. R. Burg
> American historian/writer, 1977

[Title of his gay-pride Motown hit]

I Was Born That Way.

> The Reverend Carl Bean
> American singer/songwriter, 1977

How, by the way, is one to make a noun out of that idiotic adjective *gay? A gayist? A sprite? Pollyanna?*

> Gore Vidal
> American writer, 1977

I have been to a restaurant which was, either exclusively or almost exclusively, a gay restaurant. And the worrying thing to me is that all the people looked exactly alike. There were no women to start. There were only men. They were between the ages of eighteen and twenty-eight. They had tractor boots, jeans, kitchen tablecloth shirts, and little mustaches. In England, they now have the Mexican look. They cut their mustaches (I think secretly) from underneath, and then they fold the other bit over the top. And if you see anybody with these roly-poly mustaches, you can safely stretch out your hand and shake his and say, "I see you too are queer." So, what good is this?

QUENTIN CRISP
English writer/critic, 1979

No, there is no such thing as a gay sensibility, and yes, it has an enormous impact on our culture.

JEFF WEINSTEIN
American journalist, 1980s

Homosexuality won't be accepted until it is completely seen as boring—a mundane, inconsequential part of everyday life.

QUENTIN CRISP
English writer/critic, 1980s

You know how I got gay? My mamma wasn't paying attention at the time.

LITTLE RICHARD
American rock performer, 1980s

I think that people who are gay verge on being angels, or wayward angels. Gayness is a gift.

> Hibiscus
> American performer, 1980s

Proust teaches us that every man is homosexual and every woman a lesbian.

> Charles Ludlam
> American actor/writer/director, 1980s

How many straight San Franciscans does it take to change a light bulb?

Both of them.

> American joke, 1980s

That I'm homosexual seems like a sure thing—I've associated with myself for nearly forty years.

> Mutsuo Takahashi
> Japanese poet/novelist, 1982

Homosexuality should not only be homosexual but also homoerotic.

> Mutsuo Takahashi
> Japanese poet/novelist, 1982

To be gay is to be overwhelmed with the attitudes of other people, and in order to free ourselves from that we have to put those aside and develop our own sense of what is right.

HARRY BRITT
American politician/clergyman, 1982

In the earliest era of American colonization the French and Spanish referred to native persons they called *amarionados* (effeminates); *bardaches* (catamites); *éffeminés; hermaphrodites;* and *hombres mar-iones impotentes* (impotent effeminate men). In the same era, the English referred to persons they called *amatores puerorum* (boy lovers); monsters in human shape; offending parties; sinners; Sodomites; Sodomitical boys; men who lie with men as with a woman; women who change the natural use into that which is unnatural; women who with women work wickedness; those who consent; those who do it.

JONATHAN KATZ
American historian, 1983

From childhood, gay people must be able to move back and forth skillfully between two worlds, while learning to communicate homosexually within the boundaries of a heterosexual world. Body language (use of the eyes, hips, wrists—even the little finger) and verbal cues (back when *gay* meant *happy* to most people, it meant *queer* to us) are used in a complex manner in order to establish bonds and convey information while shielding us from exposure.

ROBERT K. MARTIN
American writer/critic, 1983

Gay lives cannot be examined through straight spectacles.

ROBERT K. MARTIN
American writer/critic, 1983

I've always been quite explicit about the word "homosexual"—it is an adjective describing an action. I can't begin to see how it is an adjective that would describe a person. They talk about "gay sensibility"; I've never seen any sign of it. I've never seen any sign of "heterosexual sensibility."

> GORE VIDAL
> American writer, 1984

Ah, everything is lesbian which loves itself
I am lesbian when I really look in the mirror.

> MARTHA COURTOT
> American poet, 1984

By heterosexuals the life after death is imagined as a world of light, where there is no parting. If there is a heaven for homosexuals, which doesn't seem very likely, it will be very poorly lit and full of people they can feel pretty confident they will never have to meet again.

> QUENTIN CRISP
> English writer/critic, 1984

Everyone is basically gay. It's a question of whether they're, you know, willing.

> BOYD McDONALD
> American film critic/journalist, 1985

When I was in Sydney, a stranger, who could not have been more than seventeen years old, asked me why I was so often on television. I smirked, simpered, and admitted that I had no idea. "So you're homosexual," he said. "Big deal."

QUENTIN CRISP
English writer/critic, 1985

In this age of creeping—if not galloping—conformity, why should the gay guy allow himself to be pigeonholed any more than is absolutely necessary?

TONY LANG
American humorist, 1985

Carry a bandanna only if you are a cleaning lady. If you do carry one, make sure its color and position mean absolutely nothing.

TONY LANG
American humorist, 1985

Even I, who am fairly careful what I say, occasionally use the word "homosexual" as a substantive (though wild, pink horses could not make me turn the adjective "gay" into a noun). This slipshod use of language makes it possible for gay men to think of themselves as special people rather than as ordinary people with a special way of spending their evenings.

QUENTIN CRISP
English writer/critic, 1986

A natural extension of "the good gay life" is to create a comfortable *rural* gay life. Gay men who have fled small town America for the glitter and support of the city should consider returning to the country. . . . Country living adds an extra special dimension to our lives. Our growing numbers show that gay men *can* and *do* live everywhere.

DICK HARRISON
American journalist/rural activist, 1986

The homosexual and the heterosexual are now no longer distinct biological categories; all people are basically bisexual.

MYRIAM EVERARD
Dutch psychologist/historian, 1986

Homosexual persons should make no effort to try and join society. They should stay right where they are and give their name and serial number and wait for society to form itself around them. Because it certainly will.

QUENTIN CRISP
English writer/critic, 1987

Is there a gay sensibility? No. There is not a gay anything; we are much more diverse than that.

JUDITH GRAHN
American writer, 1987

I would define gay people as possessing a *luminous* quality of being, a differentness that accentuates the gifts of compassion, empathy, healing, interpretation and enabling. I see gay people as the *in-between ones;* those who can entertain irreconcilable differences, who are capable of uniting opposing forces as one; bridge builders who intuit the light and dark in all things.

MARK THOMPSON
American writer, 1987

Gay men have a unique potential within them to experience nature and other beings not as "objects" to be manipulated and mastered, but as "subjects," like themselves, to be respected and cherished.

DON KILHEFNER
American writer/activist, 1987

Gaiety is a great moral good and a high spiritual value, as well as being a key to the universe.

JAMES BROUGHTON
American poet/playwright/filmmaker, 1987

It was not, and is not now, in our natures and never part of our dream, to want to conquer nature . . . we were always the shy kids who walked with clouds and talked to trees and butterflies.

HARRY HAY
American writer/activist, 1987

One of the most insidious concepts used to develop our subculture has been that of *pride*. Because of the relentless nature of our oppression, gay people have had to seize upon the concept of pride in order to measure self-worth. Instilling a *sense* of pride is a justifiable component of any community, but a fixation on pride leads to isolation, inflation of individual egos and greed.

MARK THOMPSON
American writer, 1987

I don't want to think about being gay all the time. I want to have my life, my lover, my friends, and I don't want to have to spend my time being scared and angry.

HOWARD CRUSE
American cartoonist, 1988

Nebuchadnezzar was a homosexual. He would cast lots every night as to which king, whom he had captured in battle, turn it was for pederasty.

RABBI SHOLOM KLASS
American theologian/writer, 1988

The gay community encompasses people from all walks of life, all economic ranks and all political philosophies.

DELL RICHARDS
American journalist, 1988

Homosexuality is God's way of insuring that the truly gifted aren't burdened with children.

SAM AUSTIN
American composer/lyricist, 1988

GENDER

Even the hypersensitive Victorians allowed the word "gender" to be used in mixed company. It is a nice word, a cool word, a theoretical word used by grammarians rather than by sociologists. It suggests neither superiority nor inferiority. It lends itself neither to violence nor to silliness. No one is ever likely to be called a gender maniac or a gender kitten.

Nevertheless, in its own quiet way, the word is emotive.

Miss Morris, who was once Mr. Morris but who, many years ago, underwent the operation, said that her problem had never been one of sex but rather of gender. I take this statement to mean that what she wanted was less to facilitate her relationships with men than to be physically consistent—to live in a body that was the outward and visible sign of her inner idea of her soul, her character, her personality.

The differences between the sexes are purely physical. Everything else is learned. Masculinity and femininity are entirely matters of convention. They are things that we have invented. In the time of Charles the First, men wore makeup and lace on their cuffs. And there are societies where if the men fail the warrior tests, they move into the world of the women. In order for society to survive, it's very necessary to know who can fight the leopards.

The traditional differences between the sexes are vanishing. While this newest change in our society may appear to be the work of fashion *designers, deep down it is an inevitable manifestation of a law of physics. As Mr. Bronowski has stated, "The arrow of time points always in the direction of diminishing difference." In common parlance, things are getting more alike. Thus the rules of gender representation grow more lax every year.*

I come from a time when it would have been easy to compile a universally acceptable list of careers, hobbies, clothes, gestures, and even phrases that were, especially in the middle classes, deemed suitable for a man and another list appropriate to women. My own sin lay not in the performance of any particular sex act but in my being at first unable and later unwilling to forgo the expression of the feminine aspects of my nature.

To people who have a gender problem, sexual activity is only a way of affirming their dream of themselves; it is an endorsement rather than a pastime. They need praise more than anything practical, and many men who frequently put on women's clothes tell us that they have no homosexual inclinations at all.

Men . . . show their masculinity throughout their boyhood by the way they make friends with men, and the delight they take in lying beside them and being taken in their arms. And these are the most hopeful of the nation's youth, for theirs is the most virile constitution.

PLATO
Greek philosopher, 427? B.C.–347 B.C.

[Caesar is] every man's wife and every woman's husband.

CURIO THE ELDER
Roman writer, 53 B.C.

[Shouted in the senate upon the arrival of Julius Caesar, recalling his controversial affair with King Nicomedes of Bithynia]

Hail, Queen of Bithynia!

Roman Senate
49 B.C.

When nature formed you, she doubted for a moment
Whether to offer you as a girl or a boy,
But while she sets her mind's eye to settling this,
Behold! You come forth, born as a vision for all.

HILARY THE ENGLISHMAN
English poet, 1150?

Some swore he was a maid in man's attire,
For in his looks were all that men desire. . . .
His dangling tresses that were never shorn,
Had they been cut, and unto Colchos borne,
Would have allured the venus youth of Greece
To hazard more than for the Golden Fleece.

CHRISTOPHER MARLOWE
English poet/playwright, 1564–1593

All men and women woo me. There is a fragrance in their breath.

HENRY DAVID THOREAU
American writer, 1817–1862

What a good man she was, and what a kind woman.

[Regarding the death of George Sand in a letter to his friend, Gustave Flaubert]

IVAN TURGENEV
Russian novelist, 1818–1883

Madame Bovary is me.

GUSTAVE FLAUBERT
French novelist, 1821–1880

If a severe distinction of elements were always maintained the two sexes would soon drift into far latitudes and absolutely cease to understand each other.

EDWARD CARPENTER
English writer/activist, 1844–1929

All women become like their mothers. That is their tragedy. No man does. That's his.

OSCAR WILDE
Irish writer, 1854–1900
From *The Importance of Being Earnest*

The home seems to me to be the proper sphere for the man. And certainly once a man begins to neglect his domestic duties, he becomes painfully effeminate, does he not? And I don't like that. It makes men so very attractive.

OSCAR WILDE
Irish writer, 1854–1900
From *The Importance of Being Earnest*

A man is called affected, nowadays, if he dresses as he likes to dress. But in doing that he is acting in a perfectly natural manner.

OSCAR WILDE
Irish writer, 1854–1900
From "The Soul of Man Under Socialism"

[Comment regarding male homosexuality]

[They] go through in their childhood a phase of very intense but short-lived fixation on the woman (usually on the mother) and after overcoming it, they identify themselves with the woman and take themselves as the sexual object; that is, proceeding on a narcissistic basis, they look for young men resembling themselves in persons whom they wish to love as their mother has loved them. We have, moreover, frequently found that alleged inverts are by no means indifferent to the charms of women, but the excitation evoked by the woman is always transferred to the male object. They thus repeat through life the mechanism which gave origin to their inversion.

> SIGMUND FREUD
> Austrian neurologist/founder of
> psychoanalysis, 1856–1939

Among the Greeks, where the most virile men were found among inverts [homosexuals], it is quite obvious that it was not the masculine character of the boy, which kindled the love of man, but it was his physical resemblance to woman as well as his feminine psychic qualities, such as shyness, demureness and the need of instruction and help. As soon as the boy himself became a man, he ceased to be a sexual object for men and in turn became a lover of boys.

> SIGMUND FREUD
> Austrian neurologist/founder of
> psychoanalysis, 1856–1939

A spokesman for the masculine inverts stated the bisexual theory in its crudest form in the following words: "It is a female brain in a male body." But we do not know the characteristics of a "female brain." The substitution of the anatomical for the psychological is as frivolous as it is unjustified.

> SIGMUND FREUD
> Austrian neurologist/founder of
> psychoanalysis, 1856–1939

The belief that a male homosexual is necessarily a misogynist and shuns or despises women has little foundation in fact. In a measure the contrary is true. . . . Women find him understanding, intuitive, sympathetic and are thus led into close friendship with him and what might be called spurious intimacy.

> JOSEPH COLLINS
> American neurologist, 1866–1950

It takes all sorts to make a sex.

> SAKI
> (Pseudonym for Hector Hugh Munro)
> Burmese-born English writer, 1870–1916

What is sauce for the goose may be sauce for the gander, but is not necessarily sauce for the chicken, the duck, the turkey or the guinea hen.

> ALICE B. TOKLAS
> American writer, 1877–1967

The trumpeters, ranging themselves side by side in order, blow one terrific blast:—
    "THE TRUTH!"
at which Orlando woke.

He stretched himself. He rose. He stood upright in complete nakedness before us, and while the trumpets pealed Truth! Truth! Truth! we have no choice left but confess—he was a woman.

> VIRGINIA WOOLF
> English novelist, 1882–1941
> From *Orlando*

There is more difference within the sexes than between them.

IVY COMPTON-BURNETT
English author, 1892–1969

In this sable performance of sexual perversion [a drag dance] all of these men are lasciviously dressed in womanly attire, short sleeves, low-necked dresses and the usual ballroom decorations and ornaments of women, feathered and ribboned head-dresses, garters, frills, flowers, ruffles, etc., and deport themselves as women. Standing or seated on a pedestal, but accessible to all the rest, is the naked queen (a male), whose phallic member, decorated with a ribbon, is subject to the gaze and osculations in turn of all the members of this lecherous gang of sexual perverts and phallic fornicators.

CHARLES H. HUGHES
American psychologist, 1893
From *An Organization of Colored Erotopaths*

I don't feel masculinity need be forced, and extreme masculinity is something of a charade—it has a rather ludicrous quality. But a truly feminine man, like a truly masculine woman, will never do. It doesn't fit, and it's self-destructing. If the majority of heterosexuals persist in believing the stereotype, it's their misfortune; it can prevent them from honest, gratifying relationships.

CECIL BEATON
British photographer/writer/designer
1902–1980

In the female invert mentally and psychically we have a man with all
the powerful desires of a man; hence, while anatomically and socially
we have a woman, the physical development will be such as to make
the individual a good risk, and also, being classed as a female,
however much her masculine tendencies may be objectionable, she
is usually free from personal assaults, and the alcohol that she drinks
seems to have a better physiological absorbing surface.

WILLIAM LEE HOWARD
American physician/sexologist, 1906

If I were to have a play put on in which women had roles, I would
demand that these roles be performed by adolescent boys, and I
would bring this to the attention of the spectators by means of a
placard which would remain nailed to the right or left of the sets
during the entire performance.

JEAN GENET
French playwright/writer, 1910–1986

Some . . . men impersonate women on the cheap vaudeville stage, in
connection with disorderly saloons. Their disguise is so perfect, they
are enabled to sit at tables with men between the acts, and solicit for
drinks the same as prostitutes.

Chicago Vice Commission, 1911

I wish that the gays would get away from riding around in Cadillac
convertibles, especially the fat ones that look like travesties of Mae
West, and just camping it up on the streets in public view.

TENNESSEE WILLIAMS
American playwright, 1912–1983

I don't think there is such a thing as a precise sexual orientation. I think we're all ambiguous sexually.

TENNESSEE WILLIAMS
American playwright, 1912–1983

I have thought for some time, I was possessed of a female spirit, or a female soul inhabited my body. If I am a man, why is it that some men wish to have sexual relations with me? Is it a chemical affinity or a mental attraction, or something else attracts them?

PROFESSOR M
Pioneer American transvestite/educator
1914

Wilde's mother had for nine long months, before he was born, prayed continually for a girl. Her imagination dwelt upon this during nearly all her pregnancy. That her prayer was partially granted in that perplexing mixture of artist, man, woman, and egotist the world knows as Oscar Wilde was perhaps one of Nature's satires in order to show what we do when we force, through our limited laws and barbaric persecutions, these peculiar people into becoming menaces to the State through lack of capacity either to understand them or to educate them.

EDITH ELLIS
American activist/sexologist/spiritualist
1915

Girls will be boys, you know.

American postcard depicting two flappers lighting their cigarettes together
c. 1925

There's two things got me puzzled, there's two things I don't under-
    stand;
That's a mannish-acting woman, and a skipping, twistin' woman-
    acting man.

BESSIE SMITH
American singer, 1927

[Comment on seeing Truman Capote for the first time in the office of the *New Yorker*]

For God's sake! What's that?

HAROLD ROSS
American editor, 1945

[Jose Sarria urged drag queens to pin a note on their dresses with this message to foil police and prosecutors in their efforts to arrest drag queens for posing as members of the opposite sex]

"I am a boy."

JOSE SARRIA
American entertainer, 1953

An individual's gender role and orientation as boy or girl, man or woman, does not have an innate, preformed instinctive basis as some theorists have maintained. Instead the evidence supports the view that psychologic sex is undifferentiated at birth—a sexual neutrality one might say—and that the individual becomes psychologically differentiated as masculine or feminine in the course of the many experiences of growing up.

JOHN L. HAMPSON
American psychologist/sexologist, 1955

Even in the sexual sphere, the Lesbian remains essentially feminine, with the natural desires and reactions of a woman.

EDWARD DENGROVE, M.D.
American sexologist, 1957

Drag is dirty work, but someone has to do it!

CHARLES PIERCE
American entertainer, 1960s

The little boy who not only occasionally dresses up in his mother's scarves and jewelry and shoes but would wear girls' clothes exclusively if permitted to do so; who consistently avoids boys' rough-and-tumble sports, preferring to organize a group of little girls into a game in which he invariably assigns himself the role of "mother"; who is, indeed, a startling mimic of his own mother's speech patterns and mannerisms and displays a marked interest in all her domestic activities; who always sits down to urinate, and frequently expresses the wish that his penis will drop off or somehow disappear; and who repeatedly insists that he is a girl and stages uncontrollable temper tantrums when he is contradicted—this child is certainly flashing the strongest of warning signals.

HARRIET SLAVITZ
American sexologist, 1964

Once I was taken to a nightclub and I said, "I have never seen so many beautiful women in my life." My escort said, "Those aren't women, they're men." I was puzzled for days after.

HEDY LAMARR
Austrian-American actress, 1966

The man who wants to show what sex he is shouldn't wear clothes.

JOHN TAYLOR
English fashion journalist, 1966

"HOLLYWOOD SQUARES" HOST: Why do motorcyclists wear leather?

PAUL LYNDE: Because chiffon wrinkles too easily, that's why.

PAUL LYNDE
American actor, 1926–1982

I'd like any role that would stretch me, where I was credible. But I'm not about to drag myself up in leather or in chiffon.

ROCK HUDSON
American actor, 1925–1985

If Myra Myron is dead as a doornail why when I lost those ugly things it was like a ship losing its anchor and I've been sailing ever since.

GORE VIDAL
American writer, 1968
Myra Breckinridge, in *Myra Breckinridge*

So help me god she stands up and hikes up her dress and pulls down her goddam panties and shows us this scar where cock and balls should be and says quote Uncle Buck I am Myron Breckinridge unquote period paragraph I like to have fainted at the sight.

GORE VIDAL
American writer, 1968
Uncle Buck, in *Myra Breckinridge*

We didn't go for a gay concept when we put the show together. We went for a totally male, masculine celebration—that men can get up there and feel their tits and do bumps and grinds and still remain men. Narcissism is a good thing. Everyone does it, I don't care what they say. Everyone gets off on mirror-tripping.

> David "Scar" Hodo
> American singer/performer, 1970s
> Band member of the Village People

Transsexual dressing is a gay contribution to the realization that we're not a hundred percent masculine or feminine, but a mixture of hormones.

> Allen Ginsberg
> American poet, 1970s

I decided that if I was going to be labeled a queen, I would be the biggest, best queen there was.

> Jose Sarria
> American entertainer, 1970s

Said Jane to her mother, "I fear
My husband's turned into a queer.
On Sundays and Mondays
He irons all my undies,
And he secretly wears my brassiere."

> English limerick, 1970s

It's a bitch to be butch.

> American T-shirt slogan, 1970s

[YENTL'S FATHER:] Yentl—you have the soul of a man.

[YENTL:] So, why was I born a woman?

[FATHER:] Even heaven makes mistakes.

> ISAAC BASHEVIS SINGER
> Yiddish-Polish-American writer, 1970s
> Yentl and her father, in *Yentl the Yeshiva Boy*

I'm the real Yentl, except I would have known what to do with Amy Irving.

> LYNN LAVNER
> American comedian, 1988

Camp is . . . finding . . . beauty in the grotesque.

> BRUCE RODGERS
> American writer/lexicographer, 1972

Women who are camp have donated, whether they know it or not, courage and bits of wisdom to the homosexual effeminate who often imitates them.

> BRUCE RODGERS
> American writer/lexicographer, 1972

GERALDO RIVERA: Please answer me. What *are* you? Are you a woman trapped in a man's body? Are you a heterosexual? Are you a homosexual? A transvestite? A transsexual? *What* is the answer to the question?

HOLLY WOODLAWN: But, darling, what difference does it *make* as long as you look fabulous?

> HOLLY WOODLAWN
> American actress, 1976
> Dialogue with Geraldo Rivera from his
> ABC-TV talk show

Neither male nor female sexuality is limited by "genital geography," and it has been one of the greatest public relations victories of all time to convince us it was. The very naturalness of lesbianism (and homosexuality) is exactly the cause of the strong social and legal rules against it. The basing of our social system on gender difference, biological reproductive function, is barbaric and should be replaced by a system based on affirmation of the individual and support for all life on the planet.

> ANONYMOUS
> American sexologist, 1976

"Drag," as we dub it these days, is commonly thought of as a homosexual pursuit, though this is hardly the case, in our culture or any other. Ancient cultures abound in examples of transvestism, from Aztec shamans to Persian catamites. American Indian cultures often had berdashes, or crossdressers. Today, we have high school jocks getting up in drag for the senior frolics, and major comedy stars appear [in] crinolines with domestic regularity. Drag, whether it be for television comedy or ritual emasculation, occurs in too many areas of human society to be considered merely a homosexual pastime.

> DENNIS SANDERS
> American writer, 1977

For most American men—yesterday and now—the only thing worse than being a woman is to be a man who wants to be a woman. The fact that 99.9 percent of homosexualists haven't the slightest desire to be women, nor do they think of themselves as women, is still unknown out there in the wild American dark, and I can't think why.

GORE VIDAL
American writer, 1977

[Comment after his election to Mayor Moscone regarding his wish to be consulted in all official gay issues]

I'm the number-one queen in town now.

HARVEY MILK
American politician/activist, 1930–1978

Style is being yourself, but on purpose.

QUENTIN CRISP
English writer/critic, 1979

Girls got balls. They're just a little higher up, that's all.

JOAN JETT
American rock singer/musician, 1979

People already think I'm that way—homo—because of my voice, and I'm not.

[Explaining his rejection of the role of a gay dancer in the film *A Chorus Line*]

MICHAEL JACKSON
American vocalist, 1979

If little girls want to grow up and marry Michael, now they know they've got a chance.

> Press agent to Michael Jackson at a press con-
> ference called to halt rumors that Michael was
> gay and took hormones, 1980s

He didn't look feminine. Didn't look like a pretty woman. He looked like a woman who had been hit with a board and didn't get well.

[Commenting on a friend in drag]

> LITTLE RICHARD
> American rock performer, 1980s

There are easier things in this life than being a drag queen. But, I ain't got no choice. Try as I may, I just can't walk in flats.

> HARVEY FIERSTEIN
> American playwright/actor, 1981
> Arnold, in *Torch Song Trilogy*

Hermaphrodite is the term used for the anomaly of the two sex organs in one creature. Androgyne is the more symbolic word. It refers to the original unity of everything, the concept of a divine creature being both masculine and feminine and hence different from both of these.

> JAMES BROUGHTON
> American poet/playwright/filmmaker, 1982

Camp is a homosexual sensibility with a soupçon of weariness.

> NED ROREM
> American composer, 1982

A prenatal hormonal mixup can certainly produce a homosexual child. They often have delicate features, smooth and nearly hairless faces, and high-pitched voices. They walk like females and have feminine mannerisms. They love to be around women, learn to make up their faces while very young, and can do wonders with their own hair and the hair of others. They would prefer to be with girls rather than with boys.

ANN LANDERS
American columnist, 1983

The adoration of machismo is intermittent, interchangeable, between parentheses. Tonight's top is tomorrow's bottom.

EDMUND WHITE
American novelist/essayist, 1983

I do wish everyone would stop picking on drag queens; I at least continue to see them as the Saints of Bleecker Street.

EDMUND WHITE
American novelist/essayist, 1983

Thank you, America. You've got good taste, style, and you know a good drag queen when you see one.

BOY GEORGE
English rock performer, 1984

Boy George is all England needs—another queen who can't dress.

JOAN RIVERS
American comedian/television host, 1980s

Even in childhood I was mad about men in uniform.

QUENTIN CRISP
English writer/critic, 1984

Of course men will wear skirts. It is coming. Among more of the young generation the codification of what is masculinity has changed a lot. You don't wear your masculinity. You are masculine or you are not—it is not the clothes that make you masculine or feminine.

JEAN-PAUL GAULTIER
French fashion designer, 1984

Women are all female impersonators to some degree.

SUSAN BROWNMILLER
American author/feminist, 1984

All the games I played with these little girls were really only one game. We dressed up in their mothers' or even grandmothers' clothes, which we found in box rooms and attics, and trailed about the house and garden describing in piercing voices the splendors of the lives that in our imaginations we were leading.

QUENTIN CRISP
English writer/critic, 1984

The strange thing about "camp" is that it has become fossilized. The mannerisms have never changed. If I were now to see a woman sitting with her knees clamped together, one hand on her hip and the other lightly touching her back hair, I should think, "Either she scored her last social triumph in 1926 or it is a man in drag."

QUENTIN CRISP
English writer/critic, 1984

I was over thirty before, for the first time, I heard somebody say that he did not think of himself as masculine or feminine but merely as a person attracted to other persons with male sexual organs.

QUENTIN CRISP
English writer/critic, 1984

Drag should be the ultimate. And if you can afford to do the ultimate, then do the ultimate. I mean, drag should always be the best you can afford it to be.

HARVEY FIERSTEIN
American playwright/actor, 1985

I realize that I've done a lot of female impersonation. In many ways, what I did was to experiment and use it for different theatrical purposes by putting a tremendous emphasis upon the context in which it is used. Now a man or a woman might be better at evoking a specific type of personality, or it might make a specific point in the play, since gender reversal creates a Chinese box effect—we don't know what's real or unreal.

CHARLES LUDLAM
American director, 1985

When life is a real bitch again,
And my old sense of humor
    has up and gone,
It's time for the big switch again.
I put a little more mascara on.

HARVEY FIERSTEIN
American playwright/actor, 1985
Albin, in *La Cage aux Folles*

[Pee-wee Herman] argues against compulsory polarization of the sexes by summoning up a child's androgyny. Being just a kid allows Pee-wee and his pals to play with gender codes unnoticed, and therefore all the more subversively.

BARRY WALTERS
American journalist, 1985

Did Mae West invent drag queens, or did drag queens invent Mae West?

MICHAEL BRONSKI
American writer/activist, 1985

Don't call a friend a sister unless:
a) she is a woman and
b) you share at least one parent in common.

TONY LANG
American humorist, 1985

Fag hag is surely a cruel term for women who exist on a spectrum that consists of many degrees of closeness to male homosexuals—and denotes strictly the tough, party-hearty women who mystify by their insistent following of male homosexual society. We all know some. We have seen in their lives every conceivable denouement to the situation, besides.

ANDREW HOLLERAN
American literary critic, 1986

Lesbians are first and foremost women.

LAURA S. BROWN
American psychologist/sexologist, 1986

Life is a drag, you know—then you become one!

CHARLES PIERCE
American female impersonator, 1987

It's much easier for men to do drag. For a woman to be in male drag and claim that power, it's not funny. For boys to be girls is hysterical.

PEGGY SHAW
American comedian, 1988

I didn't want to mimic a woman, but to use that as a vehicle— actually, it was a way of getting out a lot of rage.

JOHN KELLY
American dancer/impersonator, 1988

Lee [Liberace] was the daddy of rhinestones and sequins—all the stuff the kids in rock are using today. He knew people called him a flaming faggot, but he didn't care. He knew that the most boring thing in the world was a piano player. He created a great game of suspense among people, making them think, *What's he going to wear this time?*

RAY ARNETT
Liberace's friend and coworker, 1988

Every man should own at least one dress, and so should lesbians.

JANE ADAMS SPAHR
American Presbyterian minister/gay
activist, 1988

Drag is not simply back, it's positively *in*.

HER IMPERIAL HIGHNESS
THE GRAND DUCHESS
TATIANA NEVAHOYDOVA
American socialite/journalist, 1988

If a woman-in-a-man's-body goes after a man, is she attracted to the same or the opposite sex? If a man-in-a-woman's-body wants a woman, is he lesbian or straight? Prejudice is only cowardice in the face of complexity.

JAY LEMKE
American anthropologist, 1988

HEALTH

ne of the madnesses that distinguish the second half of this century
from the first is its almost universal passion for exercise. Fifty years
ago the only women who took physical exercise were athletes or dancers.
Even men only carried their love of sports from their school days into
adult life for a few years before, worn out with work and marriage, they
abandoned the effort.

In those days vigorous—even brutal—games were thought by edu-
cationists to be a good substitute for sexual activity. I once asked an
accountant why he played squash in the evenings. His reply did not
contain any hint that he liked the game. He said, "If I didn't, I might
get up to all sorts of mischief." When I pointed out that mischief would
at least be more interesting than squash, he only smirked.

In those days all exercise was violent; it was even called "physical
jerks." It produced a race of hideous men who suffered early heart
attacks.

Now those quaint antics have been supplanted by gymnasium
mania—a series of slow, controlled, and carefully directed exercises.
These, instead of tearing down tissue, build it up and produce bodies,
both male and female, that are at the moment considered beautiful. Thus
the purpose of working out has changed: it is no longer enough to feel
well, it is also imperative to look well.

The gymnasiacs of Venice, in California, are so addicted to these *practices that there has arisen a nation of men who can no longer put their arms against their sides.*

Manly means beautiful. Of course, as doctors will tell you, an impressive physique is no guarantee that the possessor is in good health, but this makes no difference to gymnasiacs—not even to women. Being a picturesque invalid, which for Victorian ladies was a way of life, is out. Exercise, especially among homosexual men, is no longer instead of sex, it is employed in the service of sex.

Sex is of course a mistake. It is the last refuge of the miserable. In the past when I said this the interviewers would go back to their editors clucking that I was an antisexual reactionary. Now that so many are dying from AIDS, my views on human sexuality seem less anachronistic.

I maintain that now that sex is even less valuable, it is pursued with even greater frenzy: people are doing it more and enjoying it less.

I have had my own experience with a frightening large-scale epidemic: I lived through the Spanish influenza (and it should have taken me, for I was a skinny little thing). I have lived through other epidemics. We have only to wait this one out. It will pass.

Nature has poisoned the pleasures of love and sources of life over three-quarters of the world by a terrible disease, to which man alone is subject, and which infects only his organs of procreation.

It is not the same plague as with other diseases, which are the natural consequences of excess. It was not introduced by debauchery. The Phrynes and Laises, the Floras and Messalinas were never attacked by it. It originated in the islands where men lived together in innocence, and thence spread throughout the Old World.

> VOLTAIRE
> French philosopher/writer, 1694–1778

The sick do not ask if the hand that smooths their pillow is pure, nor the dying care if the lips that touch their brow have known the kiss of sin.

> OSCAR WILDE
> Irish writer, 1854–1900
> From *A Woman of No Importance*

Who would not rather have his son contract a bad heart or hernia than to see him a sexual pervert?

> IRVING C. ROSSE
> American medical professor, 1892

If a killing type of virus strain should suddenly arise by mutation . . . it could, because of the rapid transportation in which we indulge nowadays, be carried to the far corners of the earth and cause the deaths of millions of people.

> W. M. STANLEY
> American biochemist, 1904–1971

A pestilence isn't a thing made to man's measure; therefore we tell ourselves that pestilence is a mere bogey of the mind, a bad dream that will pass away. But it doesn't always pass away, and from one bad dream to another, it is men who pass away.

> Albert Camus
> French novelist/philosopher, 1913–1960
> From *The Plague*

Quit the baths to go home and bathe.

> Ned Rorem
> American composer, 1967

[Comment to his publicist regarding the disclosure to reporters that "Mr. Rock Hudson Has Acquired Immune Deficiency Syndrome"]

Go and give it to the dogs.

> Rock Hudson
> American actor, 1925–1985

His [Rock Hudson's] illness and death have moved the fight against AIDS ahead more in three months than anything in the past three years.

> Bruce Decker
> Chairman, California AIDS Advisory Board
> 1980s

[Caption appearing beneath a picture of a penis]

Cover me, I'm going in.

> American T-shirt slogan, 1980s

One effect of gay liberation is that sex has been institutionalized and franchised. Twenty years ago, there may have been a thousand men on any one night having sex in New York baths or parks. Now there are ten or twenty thousand—at the baths, the back-room bars, bookstores, porno theaters, the Rambles, and a wide range of other places as well. The plethora of opportunities poses a public health problem that's growing with every new bath in town.

DAN WILLIAM
American physician, 1980

Already, a Manhattan gay newspaper, *New York Native,* had published a story about the rumors of a new killer pneumonia striking gay men, but the . . . liaison with the local health department had pooh-poohed the gossip, telling the paper that the rumors were "unfounded."

RANDY SHILTS
American writer, 1981

I am encouraging the use of condoms—eroticizing the use of rubbers. When I am at a place like the Mineshaft, I make a big display of the use of a rubber—putting it on myself and my partner. I know it is not the "real thing"—it is a taste of rubber—but the overriding fear of disease affects my enjoyment of sex, and thus it is a reasonable alternative.

RICHARD LOCKE
Former porn star/gay activist, 1984

AIDS is evidence that Thanatos is not only a killing god, he is a mocking god: not only must we die, but we must die slowly, painfully, and fearfully from this new leprosy. And we are driven to wonder if man is, after all, a useless passion who dies by mere chance.

TIMOTHY MURPHY
American journalist/professor of medical
ethics, 1985

If AIDS has taught us anything, it is that we are the most tenacious, inspired, creative, caring, committed survivors on the face of this earth.

RODGER MCFARLANE
Former executive director,
Gay Men's Health Crisis, 1985

Remember: there's no such thing as a homosexual disease. When heterosexuals start having sex again, they'll get it too.

HARVEY FIERSTEIN
American actor/dramatist, 1985

At a time when some would have us go back into the closet, and others would have us focus all our energies on the crises surrounding AIDS, many of us are finding a way to continue living our lives with self-respect, dignity and verve.

ERIC E. ROFES
American writer, 1985

If gay men recognize AIDS as a sexually transmissible disease to be avoided at all costs, what good are the guidelines that include a whole set of "maybe's"?

MICHAEL HELQUIST
American journalist, 1985

No longer does one hanker for the mere image of health; one is now utterly determined to achieve and keep it. Because of the unpredictable nature of AIDS as well as the undeniable stress of this end of the century, the object now is a deep serenity bred by perfect balance, the peace of mind that manifests itself in a relaxed, fluid body and a rich, hearty soul.

PAUL REED
American writer/journalist, 1985

Along with the rest of the nation, gay men's interest in good health and general overall self-improvement is a recent phenomenon. But this new interest appears to be serious—bodybuilding is here to stay. Witness the large number of general purpose gyms as well as numerous "gay" gyms which continue to thrive and expand.

ROY F. WOOD
American writer/activist, 1985

We're not talking about a nightmare that is going to happen. It already is a nightmare.

MICHAEL LANGE
American physician/AIDS specialist, 1985

I am tired of compiling lists of the dead. They are actors and writers and designers and dancers and editors and retailers and decorators. . . . The dead are homosexuals who have contracted and will perish from AIDS. Almost everyone who knew them knows this, but there is a gentle, loving conspiracy of silence to deny reality. . . . Men are dying and we in the press cough politely and draw the curtains of discretion across the truth. Don't hurt anyone. Protect a name, a family, a reputation. A memory. So we write white lies about the cause of death. . . . Can lies *be* a cause of death?

JAMES BRADY
American journalist, 1985

We hope for a time when scientific breakthroughs and gay creativity will furnish new ways to be freely and safely sexual with other men—and gay monogamy will be a freely chosen option and not an act of self-preservation.

PHIL NASH
American writer/activist, 1986

Despite what we know about AIDS, you just think people will never die.

ANTHONY PERKINS
American actor, 1986

There is nothing wrong with being a safe-sex slut.

PAT CALIFIA
American journalist, 1987

People aren't just *dying* with AIDS, people are *living* with AIDS.

> DAVID BELL
> American activist, 1987

She was in Ward 5B, the first woman on the AIDS Ward, staring at the stark landscape outside her window and wondering how a tryst with a bisexual man several years before had brought her here.

> RANDY SHILTS
> American writer, 1987

The city recently released a long-term AIDS plan, prepared by the Interagency Task Force on AIDS, made up of seven city agencies. It is a sensible but sobering document reinforcing the perception that AIDS is the principal public health crisis of this generation.

> EDWARD I. KOCH
> Mayor of New York, 1988

I would particularly caution gays to avoid joining studies that are conducted by direct agencies of the U.S. government (such as veterans hospitals), as opposed to studies conducted in universities with review committees in place.
    The price of survival is eternal vigilance.

> ROBERT G. BODELL
> American medical researcher, 1988

In the name of humanity, I pledge to resist medical Nazism.

> CHARLES L. ORTLEB
> Publisher of *New York Native*, 1988
> From "The People's Hippocratic Oath"

AIDS is not a police issue, it's a health issue.

> RICHARD RUDELL
> Los Angeles Police Department
> administrator, 1988

Silence = Death

> AIDS rights slogan, 1988

For this much love, care, and compassion to come out of this community because of AIDS proves that we truly are a people of incredible love. We're going to be a better community because of this.

> LEONARD MATLOVICH
> American former Air Force sergeant/AIDS
> activist, 1988

Homophobia has for centuries killed us. All those projected fears and anxieties are turning back on heterosexuals and will kill them. They will die of their own prejudice because they will not pay attention to the warnings about AIDS we have given them.

> SIMON WATNEY
> American linguist/writer, 1988

I believe San Francisco will be remembered not for its losses but for its contributions to the AIDS crisis. We are a model for AIDS care and caring. People from all over the world come here to find out what we've learned and how we're coping.

> ART AGNOS
> Mayor of San Francisco, 1988

Condoms, even when used conventionally (in vaginal intercourse), have a failure rate of about 10 percent. When used for anal intercourse, they can break as often as 50 percent of the time.

If both propositions are true, having anal intercourse with a condom is rather like Russian roulette, isn't it?

> JOHN LAURITSEN
> American journalist, 1988

Doctor People Not Numbers.

> Demonstration placard slogan for
> AIDS Coalition to Unleash Power (ACT UP)
> 1988

I would hate it if a kid of mine got a blood transfusion, if my grandson had AIDS, and the community discriminated against that . . . innocent child, particularly when the [commission's] report concludes . . . that AIDS . . . cannot . . . be transmitted by ways that some had feared. . . . This is a national health problem. We're talking about children, innocent victims.

> GEORGE BUSH
> Forty-first U.S. President, 1988

The war against AIDS [is] the greatest public health emergency of our lifetimes.

> MICHAEL DUKAKIS
> Governor of Massachusetts, 1988

Put on that love glove, baby
Don't be shy.

> CHARLIE MURPHY
> American singer/songwriter, 1988

Like the Vietnam Memorial, with its endless etchings in dark marble, the Quilt is awesome in its very scope. It displays the magnitude of the epidemic. Most important, it memorializes those who are gone and records their names as personalities, not as statistics.

JOHN PRESTON
American journalist, 1988

The biggest crime involved with AIDS has been the failure to get drugs tested quickly.

MARTIN DELANEY
American activist/cofounder of Project Inform, an AIDS information organization
1988

I think in fifty years, when this catastrophe is all over, we will look back on this as our Holocaust, and we should feel the same anger that the survivors of the Holocaust still feel, and we should demand the same shame that the world should feel about the Holocaust.

PAUL MONETTE
American writer, 1988

AIDS is this generation's Vietnam.

RICHARD GOLDSTEIN
American journalist, 1988

People who get AIDS from homosexual activities or illegal drug activities certainly don't deserve—certainly won't get—my sympathy.

EMORY FOLMAR
American politician/Mayor of Montgomery
1988

[Commenting regarding panels of the Quilt]

The most devastating thing you can put on a panel is a birth date and death date. They're so young.

GINI SPIERSCH
Volunteer at the NAMES Project, 1988

HOMOPHOBIA

When homosexual people try to explain the extreme hostility felt toward them by the rest of the world, they often suggest that heterosexual men and women are trying to exorcise some latent homosexual inclinations in themselves. The gay community puts this theory forward because they seem to have difficulty believing that the whole world is not secretly homosexual; they are, in a sense, born missionaries.

I was once asked if a certain film director of my acquaintance was gay. I replied that I had seen no evidence to support such a wild surmise and added that the gentleman in question had been married three times. This observation only prompted the reply: "That merely shows how unsatisfactory his relationships with women have been." Against anyone who has made up his mind that the world is full of closet queens, you cannot hope to win.

In fact, living in a society where plenty of members of both sexes are horribly available, very few people ever have the faintest desire to experiment with sexual variations.

The sad truth about homophobia is that in the course of a lifetime, most of us accumulate a huge stockpile of resentment against the employer who never offers us promotion, against the wife who makes fun of us in front of our friends, against the children who do nothing that we ask of them. Then, one day, we are brought into contact with someone whom nobody will blame us for attacking, and suddenly all the hatred *of the black and bitter years pours out like pus from a squeezed boil.*

The attacker may adduce all sorts of arguments to justify his violence: he may say that he is inspired by religious fervor or a desire to protect his children; he may invoke the name of nature or, in modern times, cite his terror of disease, but deep down, he has no definable motive. His fury is blind.

No argument, no legislation, no education, no pleas for mercy can avert his rage. This is an aspect of communal life that minorities have always been compelled to endure.

It is better to be hated for what one is than to be loved for what one isn't.

ANDRÉ GIDE
French novelist/critic, 1869–1951

I can remember that not so long ago George M. Cohan, and other super he-men, regarded the wristwatch as an emblem of pansiness.

PERCY HAMMOND
American theater critic, 1873–1936

Of the abnormal sexual manifestations that one encounters, none, perhaps, is so enigmatical and to the average person so abhorrent as homosexuality. I have discussed this subject with many broad-minded, intelligent professional men and laymen and have been surprised to hear how utterly disgusted they become at the very mention of the name and how little they understand the whole problem. . . . *Tout comprendre c'est tout pardonner* [To understand everything is to forgive everything]. . . . I have met and studied a large number of homosexuals and have been convinced that a great injustice is done to a large class of human beings, most of whom are far from being the degenerates they are commonly believed to be.

A. A. BRILL
American psychiatrist, 1874–1948

What the public really loathes in homosexuality is not the thing itself but having to think about it.

E. M. FORSTER
English author, 1879–1970

One thing is true. Our loves bear as fair and noble flowers, incite to as praiseworthy efforts as does the love of any man for the woman of his affections. There are the same sacrifices, the same joy in abnegation even to the laying down of life, the same pain, the same joy, sorrow, happiness, as with men of ordinary natures. . . .

May the time soon come when science shall educate the people so that they shall rightly judge our unfortunate class, but before that time can come there will be many victims.

> Letter of anonymous merchant who emigrated to America following his arrest for homosexuality, 1882

[Comment to the press regarding the cause of lesbianism]

Defective genital organs.

> FIORELLO LA GUARDIA
> Mayor of New York, 1882–1947

There are millions of women, sedate in nature, who never heard of a lesbian, much less believing that such people exist. And many men, too.

> *Variety*
> From a review of the play *The Captive*
> October 8, 1926

[It's] worse than throwing acid in a young person's eyes.

> Judicial statement regarding *The Well of Loneliness*, by Radclyffe Hall, 1928

STUDIO ADVISER: You can't film that [*The Well of Loneliness*]. It's about lesbians.

GOLDWYN: All right. Where they got lesbians, we'll use Austrians.

> SAMUEL GOLDWYN
> American film producer, 1882–1974

The Greeks, of course, had no sexual morals whatever, and not many of any other kind, and Sappho, in these respects, was simply the product of her environment. . . . The world as she knew it did not look on homosexualism as reprehensible.

> FLORENCE FINCH KELLY
> American literary critic, 1932

Whatever the public blames you for, cultivate it: it is yourself.

> JEAN COCTEAU
> French writer/director, 1889–1963

I'm not willing just to be tolerated. That wounds my love of love and of liberty.

> JEAN COCTEAU
> French writer/director, 1889–1963

A homosexual is a female soul in a male body. "You're hitting a woman," I says.

[Her plea to New York City police to curb beatings of homosexuals]

> MAE WEST
> American actress/playwright, 1892–1980

Changing traditional attitudes toward homosexuality is in itself a mind-expanding experience for most people. But we shall not really succeed in discarding the straitjacket of our cultural beliefs about sexual choice if we fail to come to terms with the well-documented, normal human capacity to love members of both sexes.

> MARGARET MEAD
> American anthropologist, 1901–1978

About six of them came into my room, the rest stood mouthing outside. My dear, they looked *too* extraordinary. They had been having one of their ridiculous club dinners, and they were all wearing colored tail-coats—a sort of livery. "My dears," I said to them, "you look like a lot of most disorderly footmen." Then one of them, rather a juicy little piece, accused me of unnatural vices. "My dear," I said, "I may be inverted but I am not insatiable. Come back when you are *alone.*"

> EVELYN WAUGH
> English writer, 1903–1966
> Anthony Blanche, in *Brideshead Revisited*

Heterosexual society dominates [the homosexual] and leads him more or less cunningly to execution.

> JEAN-PAUL SARTRE
> French philosopher/novelist/dramatist/critic
> 1905–1980

Everyone knows about everybody in Hollywood—who sleeps with whom, who doesn't sleep, who does it standing on his head or in the dentist's chair. And some of those guys just don't like fairies.

> ROCK HUDSON
> American actor, 1925–1985

Movies were anti-gay. Movies *are* anti-gay. And movies will continue
to be anti-gay.

ROCK HUDSON
American actor, 1925–1985

People do not take the relations between men and boys seriously.
. . . They do not believe there can be tears between men. They think
we are only playing at a game and that we do it to shock them.

JAMES BALDWIN
American writer, 1924–1987

I think Americans are terrified of feeling anything. And homophobia
is simply an extreme example of the American terror that's concerned
with growing up. I never met a people more infantile in my life.
. . . It's a way of controlling people. Nobody really cares who goes
to bed with whom finally. I mean, the State doesn't really care, the
Church doesn't really care. They care that you should be frightened
of what you do. As long as you feel guilty about it, the State can rule
you. It's a way of exerting control over the universe, by terrifying
people.

JAMES BALDWIN
American writer, 1924–1987

The myth and misconception with which homosexuality has so long
been clothed must be cleared away, not to condone it but to cope with
it.

Life magazine, 1964

The love that dare not speak its name has become the neurosis that does not know when to shut up.

[On reviewing "still another fictional treatment of homosexuality"]

Time magazine, 1964

The most frequently described grievance is the prejudice most homosexuals find in heterosexuals. Antihomosexual feeling among the masses of Americans cannot be our ultimate problem; in fact straight people too are harmed by rigid, stereotyped ideas about sex and sex-roles.

CHICAGO GAY LIBERATION FOR
THE REVOLUTIONARY PEOPLE'S
CONSTITUTIONAL CONVENTION
Working Paper, 1970

One vagina plus another vagina equals zero.

DAVID REUBEN
American sexologist/author, 1972

Homosexuality isn't funny. Sometimes anything can be a source of humor, but the lives of twenty million Americans are not a joke.

GAY ACTIVISTS ALLIANCE AND
NATIONAL GAY TASK FORCE
1973

Are you disconcerted by an intelligent lesbian?

MAX FRISCH
Swiss author/architect, 1974

Gayness is even scarier to people than femaleness or blackness.

JOHN LOMBARDI
American journalist, 1975

Any woman who feels actual horror or revulsion at the thought of kissing or embracing or having physical relations with another woman should reexamine her feelings and attitudes not only about other women, but also about *herself.*

SHERE HITE
American sexologist, 1976

We will not contribute by bigotry or by silence to the ongoing persecution of our Gay daughters and sons.

PARENTS OF GAY MEN AND
LESBIAN WOMEN
1977

The heterosexual dictatorship not only recognizes its enemies but defines them in its own terms. In the last few months, I have been singled out not only as the National Fag but as the creator of a new order that means to destroy The Family, The American Empire, Capitalism, and Warm Mature Heterosexual Relationships.

GORE VIDAL
American writer, 1977

The average male in the Anglo-American world is hysterical on the subject of homosexuality. It is in the culture, a vestige of Judeo-Christianity, now in its terminal stage. Everyone knows he has homosexual instincts; and since everyone has been told from birth that if he gives way to such instincts, he is sick and evil and, in most American states, a criminal, fag-bashing is bound to be very popular for a long time.

GORE VIDAL
American writer, 1977

The Myth of the Homosexual says that there exists a person defined by sexual attraction toward people of the same biological gender. This myth serves an essential function in the preservation of culture: It denies the reality, the legitimacy, of the culture-destroying vision of the so-called homosexual, and it does this by restricting that person's essence and meaningfulness to distinct sexual acts performed with other persons of the same sex. The purpose of this myth has been, and is, to rob gay people of the power inherent in them to destroy the established order and replace it according to their vision.

MITCH WALKER
American writer, 1980s

[When asked by a male heckler, "Are you a lesbian?"]

Are you my alternative?

FLORYNCE KENNEDY
American lawyer/feminist, 1980s

Homosexuality has made the media at last. The taboos are down. [TV character] Mary Hartman tries to convert the gay next door—and fails miserably. Elton John tells *Rolling Stone* he's bi. Hollywood reveals that the real mystery behind Billy Joe's ode is you-know-what. Marcello Mastroianni and Jean-Louis Trintignant play lovers on the screen. A New York punk rock group (whose manager should know better) delights its listeners with a little ditty about a "Fifty-third and Third" hustler who takes a razor to his john. This is progress?

ROB BAKER
American writer/critic, 1980s

Lesbian invisibility is a symptom of homophobia.

EVELYN TORTON BECK
American writer/activist/professor, 1982

The men of the twenties searched themselves for vestiges of effeminacy as though for lice. They did not worry about their characters but about their hair and their clothes. Their predicament was that they must never be caught worrying about either.

QUENTIN CRISP
English writer/critic, 1984

If I had to kiss a costar—because the disease is crossing over into the straight world—I'd want assurances he doesn't have AIDS. You have to protect yourself.

JOAN RIVERS
American comedian/television host, 1984

Few words are as guaranteed to set off an explosion of fear in her belly as the word *bulldike* when it is used on a woman like a whip.

JUDITH GRAHN
American writer/activist, 1984

The rhetoric of right wing zealots is sweeping across the country, providing pious justification for violence against gays. That violence is increasing daily—from tauntings and beatings to arson and even murder.

NATIONAL GAY TASK FORCE
Advertisement, 1985

Children learn antipathy for homosexuals at home: It's as right as love. If a boy finds out he isn't drawn to girls but rather falls in love with other boys, he's learned to hate himself. He knows he is a fag. Other disrespected groups of people—Blacks, Jews, women—though they suffer stigma and injustice, learn at least a feeble sense of self-worth and belonging from their families. At worst they have a meager social place. Fags have none.

DARRELL YATES RIST
American writer/journalist, 1985

As you've probably noticed from reports in the gay press, attacks against gay people have been on the increase all over America. But did you also know that in 1981 the Radical Right spent over 2.5 million dollars a month to stir up hate primarily against lesbians and gay men through propaganda and legislation?

THE FUND FOR HUMAN DIGNITY
Advertisement, 1985

It's no wonder . . . homosexuals are so despised. They offer no comforting promise to women. They pledge no unified purpose with heterosexual men.

DARRELL YATES RIST
American writer/journalist, 1985

Someday we may feel free to live anywhere we choose. In the meantime, thank God for ghettos.

GREG JACKSON
American writer/educator, 1986

Society uses all gay people who participate in gay culture for special purposes. We are closely watched to see what constitutes the limit of a thing—too far out, too much, too low, too bad, too outrageous, too soft, too dangerous, too rough, too cultured, too aggressive, too sexual. One of the strongest measures heterosexual culture has is how close each of its members comes to being "like a faggot" or "like a dyke." We are essential to them knowing who they are.

JUDITH GRAHN
American writer, 1987

Suppose every able-bodied man between eighteen and eighty, after a period of training, was enrolled in a volunteer street patrol. He could give eight hours of his time once every two weeks to volunteer work. Such patrols could wipe crime off the streets of America, since they would outnumber the muggers, rapists and queer-bashers twenty to one.

WILLIAM S. BURROUGHS
American writer, 1987

The theme song of "The Flintstones," which has long ended with the line "We'll have a gay old time!" tra-la-la, has suddenly been changed. The famous last line now says: "We'll have a great old time!"

Melbourne *Herald*, 1987

We can't distort and corrupt gay culture to adapt to bigotry.

SARAH SCHULMAN
American novelist, 1988

Women aren't nearly as hysterical about lesbians as men are about gays. That's because women aren't nearly as hysterical about proving they're 100 percent heterosexual. Some confused men, however, remain forever traumatized by that fateful day in ninth grade when Coach came by and patted them on the behind, and, alas, they kinda liked it.

MARGERY EAGAN
American journalist, 1988

It's tremendously empowering when you're gay to realize that you've been doing it right, and it's the bigots who are stumbling about in a fog.

HOWARD CRUSE
American cartoonist, 1988

[On the movie version of his play *Torch Song Trilogy*]

Matthew [Broderick] is a teen idol now, and to have the audience love him in the first part of the film and then watch him get bashed to death by teenagers for being a faggot will be devastating. Matthew usually gets $3½ million a film, and he did this film for virtually no money because he believes so much in it.

HARVEY FIERSTEIN
American playwright/actor, 1988

The fellow who dies of sodomy is no more special than the fellow who dies of two packs of cigarettes a day. Let us apportion our tears, and our tax dollars, with some sense of proportion.

JAMES J. KILPATRICK
American politician, 1988

We say, "Praise God for AIDS."

JOHN BAUMGARDNER
American Grand Dragon/Ku Klux Klan,
Florida Chapter, 1988

"Queer" is frequently loaded with hatefulness by the person who utters it. There's nothing to be gained by gays sugarcoating hatred. "Queer" should be a reminder of society's disdain for gays. There are better names to call ourselves.

DAVE WALTER
American journalist, 1988

At family dinners, when talk turns to "fags," I often wonder what would happen if—instead of staring silently into my mashed potatoes—I were to make a plea for gay rights, finally solving the mystery of my "celibacy."

> JAMES MERRETT
> American journalist, 1988

More black gay men, with the education and the skills, should devote their time and energy toward reclaiming inner-city neighborhoods, thereby helping to eliminate some of the black homophobia and setting an example for the community. That is far more important than trying to force white people to love and/or accept us.

> CHARLES MICHAEL SMITH
> American journalist, 1988

The greater the horror of homosexuals, the easier it is to make young men sweat and fight by calling them "sissy" or "fag." The cult of homophobia helps insure that poor, uneducated, young males provide Muscle for work and for war. It also keeps them out of art, culture, college, and white-collar jobs—by their own "choice."

> JAY LEMKE
> American anthropologist, 1988

[Quilt panel submitted to NAMES Project honoring anonymous person who died of AIDS]

I have decorated this banner to honor my brother.
Our parents did not want his name used publicly.
The omission of his name represents
the fear of oppression that AIDS victims and their families feel.

> ANONYMOUS
> 1988

Homophobia, for all the changes in society and human discourse since the Middle Ages, remains fervent.

ANDREW HOLLERAN
American literary critic, 1988

LOVE AND MARRIAGE

here was once a singer called Miss Cogan who became identified with a ditty that told us that "love and marriage go together like a horse and carriage." This is a charming sentiment but far from the truth. If, in this context, we are using the word "love" to signify romantic attachment, then nothing kills it more surely or faster than continued propinquity.

This is a problem that causes the straight world endless misery, but for some unknown reason homosexual men and women also insist on getting mixed up in it.

Whenever a television interviewer asks one of his victims why it is so difficult for gay men to form lasting relationships, the reply is always that there are so many forces in society that keep heterosexual couples together and an even greater number that drive homosexual pairs apart. In other words, excuses are made. No one ever replies, "I am happy to say that, owing to our volatile temperaments and our disengagement from society, we are free forever from the damp, dark prison of eternal love."

The desire of some homosexual couples to encumber their friendships with the hideous trappings of normality is due to their being unable to rid themselves of an exile's view of that other world. Standing with his nose pressed against the cold windowpane of heterosexuality, the outsider imagines that everything on the other side of the glass is peaceful, permanent, cozy. I've terrible news for him: Inside, they're longing to get out.

I am glad to say that I have never been edged into lending my gracious presence to one of these pseudo-wedding ceremonies. Therefore I cannot say whether the officiating priest actually offers the homosexual pair the sacrament of marriage, but even if he only offers to bless the couple's friendship, I cannot imagine how he squares such an action with the precepts of any branch of organized Christianity.

I've been told that my views on cohabitation are insensitive, so let me add that if you do find yourself stuck with someone, you might as well muddle through. Do not think, however, that this is the way in which you will be happy. If you do, you are intending to use your partner. You must always intend to sacrifice yourself. You must say, "I feel I have all sorts of things to give to this relationship and I will do my utmost to give them. I expect to die fulfilled—not happy."

"If you forget me, think
of our gifts to Aphrodite
and all the loveliness that we shared."

> SAPPHO
> Greek poet, 612? B.C.–580? B.C.

Human nature was originally one and we were a whole, and the desire
and pursuit of the whole is called love.

> PLATO
> Greek philosopher, 427? B.C.–347 B.C.

Far from the tender Tribe of Boys remove,
For they've a thousand ways to kindle Love.

> TIBULLUS
> Roman poet
> Between 60 and 48 B.C.–19 B.C.

A double brightness burned me: rays
There were which travelled in the gaze
Of that boy's eyes, the beams of Love;
And others from the Sun above.

> MELEAGER
> Greek poet/epigrammatist, 1st century B.C.

True love has nothing to do with women's quarters, nor will I agree
that you have ever felt *love* for women or girls, any more than flies
feel love for milk.

> PLUTARCH
> Greek biographer/essayist, 46?–120

"Tomorrow with the dawn I must attend
In yonder vale." "What for?" "Why ask? A friend
Takes him a husband there and bids a few
Be present." Wait awhile and we shall view
Such contracts formed without shame or fear
And entered on the records of the year.

> JUVENAL
> Roman satirist, 60?–140?

If a man urge me to tell wherefore I loved him, I feel it cannot be
expressed, but by answering: Because it was he, because it was my
self.

> MICHEL DE MONTAIGNE
> French essayist, 1533–1592

A woman's face with nature's own hand painted,
Hast thou the master mistress of my passion,
A woman's gentle heart but not acquainted
With shifting change as is false women's fashion,
An eye more bright than theirs, less false in rolling:
Gilding the object whereupon it gazeth,
A man in hue all hues in his controlling,
Which steals men's eyes and women's souls amazeth.
And for a woman wert thou first created,
Till nature as she wrought thee fell a-doting,
And by addition me of thee defeated,
By adding one thing to my purpose nothing.
　　But since she pricked thee out for women's pleasure,
　　Mine be thy love and thy love's use their treasure.

> WILLIAM SHAKESPEARE
> English playwright/poet, 1564–1616

I am neither a god nor an angel, but a man like any other, and confess
to loving those dear to me more than other men. . . . Christ had his
John, and I have my Steenie.

KING JAMES I
King of Scotland and Great Britain
1566–1625

And what is she (quoth he) whom thou do'st love?
    Looke in this glasse (quoth I) there shalt thou see
    The perfect forme of my faelicitie.
When, thinking that it would strange Magique prove,
    He open'd it: and taking of the cover,
    He straight perceav'd himselfe to be my Lover.

RICHARD BARNFIELD
English .poet, 1574–1427

Never did Marriage such true Union find,
Or men's desires with so glad violence bind;
For there is still some tincture left of Sin,
And still the Sex will needs be stealing in.

ABRAHAM COWLEY
English poet, 1618–1667

I thee, both as man and woman, prize;
For a perfect love implies
Love in all capacities.

ABRAHAM COWLEY
English poet, 1618–1667

Change everything except your loves.

> VOLTAIRE
> French author/philosopher, 1694–1778

I would not part from her side, but ate and slept, walked and mused and read, with my arm locked in hers, and with her breath fanning my cheek. . . . O precious inebriation of the heart! O preeminent love!

> CHARLES BROCKDEN BROWN
> American novelist, 1771–1810
> The female narrator, in *Ormond*

Oh! What a wonderful mixture of emotions transports me! I feel nature! I feel friendship! How strongly my entire soul rejoices in both! Truly Emilia, I believe friendship is stronger than love!

> ELISABETH MARIA POST
> English novelist, 1775–1812
> Eufrosyne to Emilia, from *Het Land,* or
> *The Countryside*

Listen, lady,
    For very womanhood, We are of one age,
One country, and one sex; defenseless women!
    . . . Oh, shall we not be true
To one another? Save me! Save me! Once
Thou lovedst thine own poor handmaid!

> MARY RUSSELL MITFORD
> English novelist/playwright, 1787–1855
> Inez to Constance, in *Inez de Castro*

The power of love consists mainly in the privilege that Potentate possesses of coining, circulating, and making current those false-hoods between man and women, that would not pass for one moment, either between woman and woman, or man and man.

> CHARLES CALEB COLTON
> English writer, 1780?–1832

My love and ambition for you often seems to be more like that of a mother for a son, or a father for a daughter (the two fondest of natural emotions) than the common bonds of even a close friendship between two women of different ages and similar pursuits. . . . It is a strange feeling, but one of indescribable pleasure.

> MARY RUSSELL MITFORD
> English novelist/playwright, 1787–1855
> From a letter to Elizabeth Barrett

I could love anything on earth that appeared to wish it.

> LORD BYRON
> English poet, 1788–1824

There are two hearts whose movements thrill
  In unison so closely sweet,
That pulse to pulse responsive still,
  They both must heave, or cease to beat.

There are two souls whose equal flow
  In gentle stream so calmly run,
That when they part—they part?—ah no!
  They cannot part—those souls are one.

> LORD BYRON
> English poet, 1788–1824

Ours too the glance none saw beside;
   The smile none else might understand;
The whisper'd thought of hearts allied,
   The pressure of the thrilling hand;
The kiss so guiltless and refin'd
   That Love each warmer wish forbore;
Those eyes proclaim'd so pure a mind,
   Ev'n passion blush'd to plead for more.

LORD BYRON
English poet, 1788–1824

The nature of love and friendship is very little understood, and the distinction between them ill-established. This latter feeling—at least, a profound and sentimental attachment to one of the same sex—often precedes the former. It is not right to say, merely, that friendship is exempt from the smallest alloy of sensuality.

PERCY BYSSHE SHELLEY
English poet, 1792–1822

Sweet boy, gentle boy,
Don't be ashamed, you are mine forever:
The same rebellious fire is in both of us,
We are living one life.

I am not afraid of mockery:
Between us, the two have become one,
We are precisely like a double nut
Under a single shell.

ALEXANDER PUSHKIN
Russian poet/novelist/playwright
1799–1837

A glimpse through an interstice caught,
Of a crowd of workmen and drivers in a bar-room around the stove
late of a winter night, and I unremark'd seated in a corner,
Of a youth who loves me and whom I love, silently approaching and
seating himself near, that he may hold me by the hand,
A long while amid the noises of coming and going, of drinking and
oath and smutty jest,
There we two, content, happy in being together, speaking little,
perhaps not a word.

> WALT WHITMAN
> American poet, 1819–1892

The divine magnet is on you, and my magnet responds. Which is the
biggest? A foolish question—they are *One.*

[From a letter to Nathaniel Hawthorne]

> HERMAN MELVILLE
> American novelist, 1819–1891

Already I feel that Hawthorne had dropped germinous seeds into my
soul. He expands and deepens down, the more I contemplate him;
and further and further, shoots his strong New England roots into the
hot soil in my Southern soul.

> HERMAN MELVILLE
> American novelist, 1819–1891

The one I love most lay sleeping by me under the same cover in the
   cool night
In the stillness in the autumn moonbeams his face was inclined
   toward me,
And his arm lay lightly around my breast—and that night I was
   happy.

WALT WHITMAN
American poet, 1819–1892

Doubtless I could not have perceived the universe, or written one of
   my poems, if I had not freely given myself to comrades, to love.

WALT WHITMAN
American poet, 1819–1892

Her breast is fit for pearls,
But I was not a "Diver"—
Her brow is fit for thrones
But I have not a crest.
Her heart is fit for *home*—
I—a Sparrow—build there
Sweet of twigs and twine
My perennial nest.

EMILY DICKINSON
American poet, 1830–1886

Full well I knew, though decency forbad
The same caresses to a rustic lad;
Love, love it was, that made my eyes delight
To have his person ever in my sight.

> ANONYMOUS
> English poet, 1833
> From "Don Leon," a purported
> autobiographical poem of Byron's life

       Oh! 'tis hard to trace
The line where love usurps tame friendship's place.
Friendship's the chrysalis, which seems to die,
But throws its coils to give love wing to fly.

> ANONYMOUS
> English poet, 1833
> From "Don Leon," a purported
> autobiographical poem of Byron's life

Other attachments followed, so much less restful than friendships,
that I cannot fairly call them by that consoling name. Their objects
were good women all, thank God! and the only trouble was not that
we loved unwisely, but too well.

> FRANCES E. WILLARD
> American educator/reformer, 1839–1898

The loves of women for each other grow more numerous each day, and I have pondered much why these things were. That so little should be said about them surprises me, for they are everywhere. . . . There is no village that has not its examples of "two hearts in counsel," both of which are feminine. Oftentimes these joint proprietors have been unfortunately married, and so have failed to "better their condition" until, thus clasping hands, they have taken each other "for better or for worse."

> FRANCES E. WILLARD
> American educator/reformer, 1839–1898

[Comment in his journal about Percy Granger, American composer]

I love him like I love a young woman.

> EDVARD GRIEG
> Norwegian composer, 1843–1907

Now when I am near to you, dear friend,
    Passing out of myself, being delivered—
  Through those eyes and lips and hands, so loved, so
ardently loved,
    I am become free;
  In the sound of your voice I dwell
As in a world defended from evil.

> EDWARD CARPENTER
> English writer/activist, 1844–1929

It is often said how necessary for the ordinary marriage is some public recognition of the relation, and some accepted standard of conduct in it. May not, to a lesser degree, something of the same kind be true of the homogenic attachment? It has had its place as a recognized and guarded institution in the elder and more primitive societies; and it seems quite probable that a similar place will be accorded to it in the societies of the future.

EDWARD CARPENTER
English writer/activist, 1844–1929

Unwilling as the world at large is to credit what I am about to say, and great as are the current misunderstandings on the subject, I believe it is true that Uranian men are superior to the normal men in this respect—in respect for their love-feeling—which is gentler, more sympathetic, more considerate, more a matter of the heart and less one of mere physical satisfaction than that of ordinary men.

EDWARD CARPENTER
English writer/activist, 1844–1929

The sight of a beautiful youth awakens astonishment in the lover, and opens the door to his heart to the delight which contemplation of this loveliness affords. Love takes possession of him so completely that all his thought and feeling goes out in it. If he finds himself in the presence of the beloved, he rests absorbed in gazing on him. Absent, he thinks of nought but him.

Albanian mountain tribesman
1853

For my part you are always in me. Are we no longer to live happily together? Only follow the feelings of your heart.

ARTHUR RIMBAUD
French poet, 1854–1891

The only difference between a caprice and a life-long passion is that
the caprice lasts a little longer.

OSCAR WILDE
Irish writer, 1854–1900

Those who are faithful know only the trivial side of love; it is the
faithless who know love's tragedies.

OSCAR WILDE
Irish writer, 1854–1900

One should always be in love. That is the reason one should never
marry.

OSCAR WILDE
Irish writer, 1854–1900

A man can be happy with any woman as long as he does not love her.

OSCAR WILDE
Irish writer, 1854–1900

"The love that dare not speak its name" in this century is such a great affection of an elder for a younger man as there was between David and Jonathan, such as Plato made the very basis of his philosophy, and such as you find in the sonnets of Michelangelo and Shakespeare. It is that deep, spiritual affection that is as pure as it is perfect. It dictates and pervades great works of art like those of Shakespeare and Michelangelo, and those two letters of mine, such as they are. It is in this century misunderstood, so much misunderstood it may be described as the "love that dare not speak its name," and on that account of it I am placed where I am now. It is beautiful, it is fine, it is the noblest form of affection. There is nothing unnatural about it. It is intellectual, and it repeatedly exists between an elder and a younger man, when the elder man has intellect, and the younger man has all the joy, hope and glamour of life before him. That it should be so the world does not understand.

[From his trial for sodomy]

OSCAR WILDE
Irish writer, 1854–1900

To love oneself is the beginning of a life-long romance.

OSCAR WILDE
Irish writer, 1854–1900
From *Phrases and Philosophies for the Use of the Young*

EDWARD CARSON, prosecutor at Wilde's trial: Have you ever adored a
young man madly?
OSCAR WILDE: No, not madly; I prefer love—that is a higher form.

OSCAR WILDE
Irish writer, 1854–1900

You never know a man until you know how he loves.

SIGMUND FREUD
Austrian neurologist/founder of
psychoanalysis, 1856–1939

He would not stay for me; and who can wonder?
  He would not stay for me to stand and gaze.
I shook his hand and tore my heart in sunder
  And went with half my life about my ways.

A. E. HOUSMAN
English poet/scholar, 1859–1936

Thus twice hath friendship barred the way
  to what I hoped for most of all;
But what is love, if it obey
  not friendship's call?

EDWARD PERRY WARREN
American art historian/collector 1860–1936

Years and years I have fear'd the shame
  And the cruel speech of the world.
But over our heads in the darkness now
  Is the banner of love unfurl'd,
(Lean closer, cling to me, kiss my lips,
  Our love can despise the world.)

GABRIEL GILLET
English poet, 1863– ?

Suspicious of my simplest acts I grow;
  I doubt my passing words, however brief;
  I catch his glances feeling like a thief.
Perchance he wonders why I shun him so,—
It would be strange indeed if he should know
  I love him, love him, love him past belief!

JOHN GAMBRIL NICHOLSON
English poet, 1866–1931

I fell a-weeping and I cried, "Sweet youth,
Tell me why, sad and sighing, thou dost rove
These pleasant realms? I pray thee speak me sooth
What is thy name?" He said, "My name is Love."
Then straight the first did turn himself to me
And cried, "He lieth, for his name is Shame,
But I am Love, and I was wont to be
Alone in this fair garden, till he came
Unasked by night; I am true Love, I fill
The hearts of boy and girl with mutual flame."
Then sighing said the other, "Have thy will,
I am the Love that dare not speak its name."

LORD ALFRED DOUGLAS
English poet/editor, 1870–1945

What in God's name does one call this sensibility if it be not love?
. . . This incredible feeling of sisterhood.

DOROTHY THOMPSON
American journalist, 1894–1961

Love of man for woman waxes and wanes.
Love of brother for brother
is as steadfast as the stars.

> HERBERT BRENON, 1926
> Opening title of *Beau Geste*

I caught sight of a splendid Misses. She had handkerchiefs and kisses. She had eyes and yellow shoes she had everything to choose and she chose me. In passing through France she wore a Chinese hat and so did I. In looking at the sun she read a map. And so did I. In eating fish and pork she just grew fat. And so did I. In loving a blue sea she had a pain. And so did I. In loving me she of necessity thought first. And so did I. How prettily we swim. Not in water. Not on land. But in love.

[About Alice B. Toklas]

> GERTRUDE STEIN
> American writer, 1874–1946

[Maurice and his friend Clive] were concerned with a passion that few English minds have admitted, and so created untrammelled. Something of exquisite beauty arose in the mind of each at last, something unforgettable and eternal, but built of the humblest scraps of speech and from the simplest emotions.

"I say, will you kiss me?" asked Maurice, when the sparrows woke in the eaves above them, and far out in the woods the ring-doves began to coo.

> E. M. FORSTER
> English author, 1879–1970
> Narrator, in *Maurice*

We that were friends tonight have found
    A fear, a secret, and a shame:
I am on fire with that soft sound
    You make, in uttering my name.

Forgive a young and boastful man
    Whom dreams delight and passions please,
And love me as great women can
    Who have no children at their knees.

                JAMES ELROY FLECKER
                English poet/playwright, 1884–1915

Oh! I want to put my arms around you, I ache to hold you close. Your ring is a great comfort. I look at it & think she does love me or I wouldn't be wearing it.

[From a letter to her lover, Lorena Hickock]

                ELEANOR ROOSEVELT
                American First Lady, 1884–1962

Long-term relationships between two males are notably few.

                ALFRED KINSEY
                American zoologist/sociologist/sexologist
                1894–1956

[From a letter to his friend, Wilbur Underwood]

Saturday night I at last was taken into the arms of love again! Seldom have I had such affection offered me. An athlete—very strong—20 only—dark-haired—distantly Bohemian. I hope it will last a while—I deserve a little kindness and he *was* so kind!

                HART CRANE
                American poet, 1899–1932

[To his roommate and friend, Gilda]

The actual facts are so very simple. I love you. You love me. You love Otto. I love Otto. Otto loves you. Otto loves me.

> NOEL COWARD
> English actor/playwright/composer
> 1899–1973
> Leo, in *Design for Living*

Marriage! What a strange word to be applied to two men! Can't you hear the hell-hounds of society baying full pursuit behind us? But that's just the point. We are beyond society. We've said thank you very much, and stepped outside and closed the door.

> FRANCIS OTTO MATTHIESSEN
> English writer/educator, 1902–1950

Was it possible for love and friendship to be blended into one? But before I had time to even ask the question it was answered. What is this wistful yearning I feel on these gray foggy mornings? It's not fog in my throat but an inchoate surge from my heart. What makes this new sensitive tingling in the tips of my fingers and on my lips? It isn't the cold. It's love.

> FRANCIS OTTO MATTHIESSEN
> English writer/educator, 1902–1950

[Comment regarding Beaton's relationship with Mick Jagger]

We loved each other—not carnally. But we loved what the other had. There was a fascination, a mutual one. Mick was lots of fun. He loved dressing up, and like me, he was iconoclastic in his work but somewhat formal underneath. . . . Everyone says he's bisexual. He *wants* you to think so, yet I, who am in a position to know the truth, have never heard or seen anything which would prove it.

> CECIL BEATON
> British photographer/writer/designer
> 1902–1980

The only abnormality is the incapacity to love.

> ANAÏS NIN
> French writer, 1903–1977

If equal affection cannot be,
Let the more loving one be me.

> W. H. AUDEN
> American poet, 1907–1973

I could not make love to boys without loving them.

> JEAN GENET
> French playwright/writer, 1910–1986

Claire, if I speak of the smell of garrets, it is for memory's sake. And of the twin beds where two sisters fall asleep, dreaming of one another.

> JEAN GENET
> French playwright/writer, 1910–1986
> Claire to Solange, in *The Maids*

Why I think that's the most contemptible thing you could do—marry a woman and use her as a cloak to cover what you are.

> MAE WEST
> American actress/playwright, 1927
> Grayson, in *The Drag*

I have frequently given my best sexual performance with people I didn't love, in fact rather despised. I have fucked the arses off aging queens quite easily, but found a beautiful young boy often too difficult to come, because I loved him too much.

> JOE ORTON
> English playwright, 1933–1967

Went to dinner with Nigel. "I was once very nearly married to a lesbian," he confessed over the meal, as we wearily waited for the menu. "She turned me down, fortunately."

> JOE ORTON
> English playwright, 1933–1967

A multitude of men who love only men marry and become fathers. Fed to satiety with the overflowing bounty of woman in a single wife, they don't so much as lay a hand on another woman. Among the world's devoted husbands men of this kind are not few. If they have children, they become more mother than father to them. Some women prefer a peaceful life, and such men.

> YUKIO MISHIMA
> Japanese novelist, 1925–1970
> Shunsuke, in *Thirst for Love*

Admittedly *some* are best served when the struggle for power narrows to but one other person and the duel endures for a lifetime as mate attempts to destroy mate in that long wrangling for supremacy which is called marriage. Most human beings, however, prefer the short duet, lasting anywhere from five minutes with a stranger to five months with a lover.

> GORE VIDAL
> American writer, 1968
> Myra Breckinridge, in *Myra Breckinridge*

[Comment regarding his experience as chapel organist in a prison]

[He] needed love. That it was homosexual love was, in my opinion, of no importance. It was the only variety available and the need was crucial.

So we became lovers.

> JAMES BLAKE
> American writer, 1970

All heterosexual relationships are corrupted by the imbalance of power between men and women.

> JANIS KELLY
> American writer/activist, 1972

I don't like the word love. It's like patriotism. It's like the flag. It's the last refuge of scoundrels. When people start talking about what wonderful, warm, deep emotions they have and how they love people, I watch out. Somebody is going to steal something.

> GORE VIDAL
> American writer, 1973

Too many people, both straight and gay, see gay relationships as sad, necessarily transient sadomasochistic parodies of heterosexual marriages which cause nothing but unhappiness to the parties involved. This is simply not true. . . . Same-sex relationships are no more problematic but no easier than any other human relationships. They are in many ways the same and in several ways different from heterosexual relationships but in themselves are no less possible or worthwhile.

CHRISTOPHER LARKIN
American film director, 1973

My impression is that the only people interested in marriage are Catholic priests and homosexualists. Most enlightened heterosexuals now avoid marriage in much the same way as Count Dracula steers clear of garlic.

GORE VIDAL
American writer, 1977

Since those who believe in romantic love suffer so much anyway, I would not dream of adding to their sufferings.

GORE VIDAL
American writer, 1977

All *matriarchal* societies are anti-sexual in general and specifically anti-homosexual. It's to the advantage of women. They want to get married, for Christ's sake.

WILLIAM S. BURROUGHS
American novelist, 1978

Every morning, you should say to yourself (preferably out loud), "Other people are a mistake." No, I withdraw that remark, it might be thought sweeping. Say to yourself, "Concern with other people is a mistake." Now, I know this is not what most people teach, but I am trying to spare you the traditional scramble for mutual self-sacrifice.

> QUENTIN CRISP
> English writer/critic, 1979

Love is the extra effort that we make in our dealings with those whom we do not like.

> QUENTIN CRISP
> English writer/critic, 1979

As a test of whether you're still in touch with somebody else, being loved can never be a patch on being murdered. That's when somebody has really risked his life for you.

> QUENTIN CRISP
> English writer/critic, 1979

Is there life after marriage? The answer is no. The constant proximity of another person will cramp your style in the end: unless that person is somebody you love, and then that burden will become unbearable at once.

> QUENTIN CRISP
> English writer/critic, 1979

When I say you must live alone, I am not trying to curtail your sex life. All I'm trying to do is to snatch the straw from your beak and prevent all this nesting.

QUENTIN CRISP
English writer/critic, 1979

I am so *bored* with normal-looking people, whether they're gay or not. And besides being boring, it's a big lie to tell all those people out there that what we want is the same lifestyle as theirs, the same suburb, the same house; to adopt children and live like *them.* It's just a big lie. It's the way we dress ourselves up to make ourselves more comfortable with our straight friends.

RICHARD BENNER
American director, 1979

No scientific differentiation has ever been proposed, nor is it easy to conceive of an experiment which might be performed to determine whether one person's love for another was friendly or erotic. From a phenomenological point of view, it seems likely that "friendship" and "love" are simply different points on a scale measuring a constellation of psychological and physiological responses to other humans.

JOHN BOSWELL
American historian, 1980

Today, after many years of a successful marriage, with a happy home and with children, and with a firm bond of friendship that has developed with a man who has been an inspiring person in my life, I sit down to relate what it means to be a homosexual. This is not the thinking of a bitter and unhappy person. It is the accumulated experience and outlook of one who has been through the struggle with himself and with society.

DONALD WEBSTER CORY
American writer/pioneer activist, 1980s

One of the most frequent myths created by both the heterosexual and gay worlds is that gay lovers don't remain together. It is shocking how many young gay men believe this to be true.

CHARLES SILVERSTEIN
American writer, 1981

There are two general categories of gay men—excitement seekers and home builders. Not all gay men are totally one or the other (in fact, most gay men are a combination of both), but each gay man is usually motivated more in one direction than the other.

CHARLES SILVERSTEIN
American writer, 1981

Belonging is a form of identification. One may identify as a lesbian, but lesbianism has little reclaimed history and no traditions. There are no celebrations to mark the stages in the life of a lesbian, her initiation or her union with another, no coming-of-age rituals, weddings, or lesbian gatherings at the birth of a child. Even at her death, a lesbian's life-long commitment to another woman may be contested or made invisible by omission.

SAVINE TEUBAL
English writer/historian, 1982

The average woman, unless she is particularly ill-favored, regards loving and being loved as a normal part of life. If a man says he loves her she believes him. Indeed some women are convinced they are adored by men who can be seen by all to be running in the opposite direction. For homosexuals this is not so. Love and admiration have to be won against heavy odds.

QUENTIN CRISP
English writer/critic, 1984

I have seen lesbian plums which cling to each other
in the tightest of monogamous love
and I have watched lesbian pumpkins
declare the whole patch their playground.

MARTHA COURTOT
American poet, 1984

All liaisons between homosexuals are conducted as though they were between a chorus girl and a bishop. In some cases both parties think they are bishops.

QUENTIN CRISP
English writer/critic, 1984

Spinsterhood is a Gay office that has passed through the transition of women's central and controlling position in societies to the patriarchal systems of today's world. Because the office always allows women to avoid marriage and establish or maintain an independent economic base, it has been of primary importance to the survival of women's freedom, hope, and the ability to express ourselves outside of family life.

JUDITH GRAHN
American writer/activist, 1984

Don't be 100 percent certain about the differences between a Trick, a Number, a Thing, a Relationship and a Lover. Get them confused once in a while. Try occasionally to have a Thing with a Lover or a Relationship with a Trick.

> TONY LANG
> American humorist, 1985

The primary difference between a heterosexual marriage and a homosexual relationship is that the law covers the operation of one and has nothing to do with the other.

> MARK SENAK
> American attorney, vice chairperson
> AIDS Resource Center, Inc., 1985

Visible gay couples are rare role models and should strive to present the best possible impression.

> BRYAN MONTE
> American writer/editor, 1986

After all, straight people shouldn't have a monopoly on Bloomingdale's bridal registry. I'd love to have a few place settings of Fitz & Floyd china on my breakfront.

> CRAIG G. HARRIS
> American writer/producer, 1986

Nowhere is it said that he who lives alone cannot have a lover. There are perfectly logical and rational reasons for lovers to maintain separate residences. The reasons may be professional and they may be personal.

> JOHN E. JONES
> American writer/activist, 1986

If you do have a hankering to be formally bonded, don't be ashamed. Go for it! Chart out a game plan, find that man of your dreams and claim him.

CRAIG G. HARRIS
American writer/producer, 1986

Gay-centered eros, which illuminates life with its own peculiar light, frees gay people from certain tasks and obligations (which seem assigned at birth to others), allowing them to expand on life in different ways.

MARK THOMPSON
American writer, 1987

In calling ourselves gay we say that love is central, and after the shame and guilt, and yes after the anger, love remains a word we can speak unabashed while others cringe at its too-telling power. We are the subjects of the power of love.

AARON SHURIN
American writer, 1987

Sure, a lot of gays who live in the mainstream have friends and family who care just as much about them. But there's something intangibly unique about the constant caring and loving that gays living in Community give to one another. It is a love that overcomes diverse backgrounds—a love that transcends disagreements. But most of all, it is a love that survives our ephemeral bonds to this planet.

RICHARD OSBORNE
American journalist, 1988

POLITICS AND THE LAW

Classically, the words "policy," "politics," and even "polite" all describe the art of living in a city. Contrary to popular belief, the Greeks never mastered this skill; they were a ludicrously quarrelsome and litigious bunch, forever suing one another over the most trivial matters.

To us, "politics" means nothing more than the ability to make the inevitable appear to be a matter of wise human choice.

In spite of this we are always appealing to our congressmen and our senators to espouse our causes and solve our problems. Inevitably those who most often ask for political help are the world's losers because they have the greatest difficulty living in close proximity to their fellow men, but it is a grave mistake to imagine that a new law, enacted in the teeth of general opposition, will alter public opinion; the opposite is true. It is a shift in public opinion that very gradually modifies the law. If any minority, by sheer persistence or by force of personality in one of its leaders, succeeds in altering some statute, the reform will lapse or become a rule that everyone knows but of which nobody takes any notice.

Homosexual men and women seem to be the species least willing to accept this fact. Their idealism and their altruistic zeal are to be commended, but it is quite unrealistic to suppose that easier relations with the rest of the world will result from the shaking of fists in the face of the public. Anger begets anger; that is one of nature's unalterable laws. In order to avoid living amid constant antagonism, it is as well to accept that none of us has rights; if we all got what we deserve, we would starve.

Politics and, to some extent, the law try to work on the principle that it is possible to bribe, bully, or bludgeon people into being virtuous or, at least, tolerant. It isn't. If anybody wants the world to become a better place, he must be better. However little this may seem, it is all that can be done.

If a man also lie with mankind, as he lieth with a woman, both of them have committed an abomination: they shall surely be put to death; their blood shall be upon them.

THE BIBLE
Leviticus 20:13, 725? B.C.

[Homosexuality] is regarded as shameful by the Ionians and many others under foreign domination. It is shameful to barbarians because of their despotic government, just as philosophy and athletics are, since it is apparently not in the best interests of such rulers to have great ideas engendered in their subjects, or powerful friendships or physical unions, all of which love is particularly apt to produce. . . . Wherever, therefore, it has been established that it is shameful to be involved in homosexual relationships, this is due to evil on the part of the legislators, to despotism on the part of the rulers, and to cowardice on the part of the governed.

PLATO
Greek philosopher, 427? B.C.–347 B.C.

I know there are some people who call them shameless; but they are wrong. It is not immodesty that leads them to such pleasures, but daring, fortitude, and masculinity; the very virtues that they recognize and welcome in their lovers—which is proved by the fact that in after years they are the only men who show any real manliness in public life.

PLATO
Greek philosopher, 427? B.C.–347 B.C.

If then one could contrive that a state or an army should entirely consist of lovers and loved, it would be impossible for it to have a better organization than that which it would then enjoy through their avoidance of all dishonor and their mutual emulation; moreover, a handful of such men, fighting side by side, would defeat practically the whole world. A lover would rather be seen by all his comrades leaving his post or throwing away his arms than by his beloved; rather than that, he would prefer a thousand times to die.

PLATO
Greek philosopher, 427? B.C.–347 B.C.

Anyone who persuades a boy who has been either abducted by him or by his corrupt accomplices to submit to lewdness . . . shall be punished with death; and if it is not accomplished, he shall be deported to some island. Their corrupted accomplices shall suffer the extreme penalty.

JUSTINIAN I
Byzantine emperor/lawmaker, 483–565?

What we are is a crime, if it is a crime to love,
For the God who made me live made me love.

BAUDRI OF BOURGUEIL
French Benedictine abbot/poet, 1046–1130

"The people with power and position in the world—
The very censors who decide what is sin and what is allowed—
These men are not immune to the soft thighs of a boy."

ANONYMOUS
Medieval poet, c. 1120.
Ganymede, in "Ganymede and Helen"

The church allows a hermaphrodite—that is, someone with the organs of both sexes, capable of either active or passive functions—to use the organ by which [s]he is most aroused or the one to which [s]he is more susceptible.

If [s]he is more active, [s]he may wed as a man, but if [s]he is more passive, [s]he may marry as a woman. If, however, [s]he should fail with one organ, the use of the other can never be permitted, but [s]he must be perpetually celibate to avoid any similarity to the role inversion of sodomy, which is detested by God.

PETER CANTOR
English religious leader, 1150?–1192

Go where we will, at ev'ry time and place,
Sodom confronts, and stares us in the face;
They ply in public at our very doors
And take the bread from much more honest Whores.
Those who are mean high Paramours secure,
And the rich guilty screen the guilty poor;
The Sin too proud to feel from Reason awe,
And Those, who practice it, too great for Law.

CHARLES CHURCHILL
English poet/satirist, 1731–1764

Paederasty became the crime of those to whom no crime could be imputed.

[Commenting on the persecutions of homosexuals during the reign of Justinian]

EDWARD GIBBON
English historian, 1737–1794
From *Decline and Fall of the Roman Empire*

[Homosexuality] is a crime, if a crime it is to be called, that produces no misery in Society.

> JEREMY BENTHAM
> English jurist/philosopher, 1748–1832
> From "Nonconformity"

What would have become of Aristides, Solon, Themistocles, Harmodius and Aristogiton, Xenophon, Cato, Socrates, Titus—the delight of Mankind, Cicero, Pliny, Trajan, Hadrian &c., &c.—these idols of their Country and ornaments of human Nature? They would have *perished on your Gibbets.*

> JEREMY BENTHAM
> English jurist/philosopher, 1748–1832
> From "Nonconformity"

I have been hunted down and persecuted these many years. . . . No truce, no respite have I experienced since the first license was taken out . . . for shooting at me.

> WILLIAM BECKFORD
> English writer (an accused homosexual,
> enduring ostracism and exile), 1760–1844

[Motto displayed on the wall in Harvey Milk's office]

All the forces in the world are not so powerful as an idea whose time has come.

> VICTOR HUGO
> French poet/dramatist/novelist, 1802–1885

[On the exile of Byron]

From native England, that endured too long
The ceaseless burden of his impious song;
His mad career of crimes and follies run,
And gray in vice, when life was scarce begun;
He goes, in foreign lands prepared to find
A life more suited to his guilty mind;
Where other climes new pleasures may supply
For that pall'd taste, and that unhallow'd eye.

ANONYMOUS
London newspaper, 1816

Love, love, clandestine love, was still my dream.
Methought there must be yet some people found,
Where Cupid's wings were free, his hands unbound
Where law had no erotic statutes framed,
Nor gibbets stood to fright the unreclaimed.

ANONYMOUS
English poet, 1833
From "Don Leon," a purported
autobiographical poem of Byron's life

Thou ermined judge, pull off that sable cap!
What! Can'st thou lie, and take thy morning nap?
Peep thro' the casement; see the gallows there:
Thy work hangs on it; could not mercy spare?
What had he done? Ask crippled Talleyrand,
Ask Beckford, Courtenay, all the motley band
Of priest and laymen, who have shared his guilt
(If guilt it be) then slumber if thou wilt;
What bonds had he of social safety broke?
Found'st thou the dagger hid beneath his cloak?
He stopped no lonely traveller on the road;
He burst no lock, he plundered no abode;
He never wrong'd the orphan of his own;
He stifled not the ravish'd maiden's groan.
His secret haunts were hid from every soul,
Till thou did'st send thy myrmidons to prowl.

> Anonymous
> English poet, 1833
> From "Don Leon," a purported
> autobiographical poem of Byron's life

There have of course been, in all ages, thousands and thousands of women who have not felt that particular sort of romance and attraction toward men, but only to their own kind; and in all ages there have been thousands and thousands of men similarly constituted in the reverse way; but they have been, by the majority, little understood and recognized. Now however it is coming to be seen that they also—both classes—have their part to play in the world.

> Edward Carpenter
> American writer/activist, 1844–1929

It is indeed a burning shame that there should be one law for men and another law for women. I think there should be no law for anybody.

O SCAR W ILDE
Irish writer, 1854–1900

To be overtly homosexual, in a culture that denigrates and hates homosexuality, is to be political.

M ICHAEL B RONSKI
American journalist, 1854–1900

You've heard of my case? Don't distress yourself. All is well. The working classes are with me . . . to a boy.

[To Charles Goodhart, an actor friend]

O SCAR W ILDE
Irish writer, 1854–1900

It is a great injustice to persecute homosexuality as a crime, and cruelty too.

S IGMUND F REUD
Austrian neurologist/founder of
psychoanalysis, 1856–1939

The laws of God, the laws of man,
He may keep that will and can;
Not I: let God and man decree
Laws for themselves and not for me;
And if my ways are not as theirs
Let them mind their own affairs.
Their deeds I judge and much condemn,
Yet when did I make laws for them?

A . E . HOUSMAN
English poet/scholar, 1859–1936

In spite of all present-day clamor about . . . different rights for different individualities, there is only one law that governs mankind. . . . It is in opposition to that law . . . that we forbid the homosexualist to carry on his practices whilst we allow the heterosexualist full play. . . . The only logical . . . treatment for sexual inverts would be to allow them to seek and obtain what they require where they can, that is to say, among other inverts.

OTTO WEININGER
Pioneer sexologist, 1920s

It will probably be difficult to convince the generation succeeding ours that, when this country was at its zenith of her commercial prosperity, it was improper to utter the word homosexuality, prurient to admit its existence and pornographic to discuss the subject.

JOSEPH COLLINS
American neurologist, 1866–1950

We had a grand time— The police were perfectly lovely to us— weren't they, girls? . . . Perfectly lovely. Why the minute I walked into jail, the captain said—Well, Kate, what kind of a cell would you like to have? And I said—Oh, any kind will do, Captain, just so it has a couple of peep-holes in it. I crave fresh air.

MAE WEST
American actress/playwright, 1927
Kitchen Kate, a transvestite from *The Drag*

[Upon finding her husband, actor Sir Herbert Beerbohm Tree, dining intimately at home with a handsome young actor]

The port's on the sideboard, Herbert, and remember it's adultery just the same.

MAUD BEERBOHM TREE
English actress, 1864–1937

MILITARY MAN: Tell me, Mr. Strachey, what would you do if you saw a German soldier attempting to rape your sister?

STRACHEY: I should try and come between them.

LYTTON STRACHEY
English writer, 1880–1932

With us love is just as punishable as murder or robbery.

MARGARET ANDERSON
American editor, 1886–1973

Won't you stop this continued heckling about homosexuals and let us get on with the main work of finding Communists?

[At a meeting of the Senate]

MILLARD TYDINGS
U.S. Senator, 1890–1961

You can't hardly separate homosexuals from subversives. Mind you, I don't say every homosexual is a subversive, and I don't say every subversive is a homosexual. But a man of low morality is a menace in the government, whatever he is, and they are all tied up together.

KENNETH WHERRY
U.S. Senator, 1892–1951

I'm very militant, you know, in a quiet way.

CHRISTOPHER ISHERWOOD
English writer, 1904–1986

Generally, a fascist regime is against homosexuals. Only don't forget that in Hitler's regime the opposite was also true. The Hitler Jugend were very often homosexuals or in any case leaned toward homosexuality. So there were these two aspects. The same ambiguity exists in all examples of fascism, every time the masses are controlled, unified, or given to military exercise.

JEAN-PAUL SARTRE
French philosopher/novelist/dramatist/critic
1905–1980

[Her reply to General Eisenhower concerning his request that she seek out and uncover any lesbians in her WAC battalion]

Sir, I'll be happy to do this investigation for you but you'll have to know that the first name on the list will be mine. . . . I think the General should be aware that among those women are the most highly decorated women in the war.

> SERGEANT JOHNNIE PHELPS
> American female army officer, 1940s

Perhaps as dangerous as the actual Communists are the sexual perverts who have infiltrated our Government in recent years. The State Department has confessed that it has had to fire ninety-one of these. It is the talk of Washington and of the Washington correspondents corps.

> GUY GEORGE GABRIELSON
> American Republican National Chairman
> 1950

[J. Edgar Hoover is a] killer fruit.

> TRUMAN CAPOTE
> American writer, 1924–1984

You're not given power, you have to take it.

> HARVEY MILK
> American politician/activist, 1930–1978

Whatever happens, I shall never be alone. I shall always have a boy, a railway fare, or a revolution.

> STEPHEN SPENDER
> English writer/poet, 1955

You won't find a policeman around here; they're all over on the west side of the park chasing fairies down from trees or out of the bushes. That's all they do. That's their function.

EDWARD ALBEE
American playwright, 1959
Jerry, in *The Zoo Story*

I do not see the NAACP and CORE worrying about which chromosome and gene produces black skin or about the possibility of bleaching the Negro. I do not see any great interest on the part of the B'nai B'rith Anti-Defamation League in the possibility of solving problems of anti-Semitism by converting Jews to Christianity.

In all of these minority groups, we are interested in obtaining rights for our respective minorities as Negroes, as Jews, and as homosexuals. Why we are Negroes, Jews, or homosexuals is totally irrelevant, and whether we can be changed to whites, Christians, or heterosexuals is equally irrelevant.

FRANK KAMENY
American activist/founder of the
Washington Mattachine Society, 1960s

In the Forties the Bomb dropped. In the Forties the entire planet was threatened biologically. In the Forties there was a recovery from a total breakdown of all morality in the concentration camps. For those of us who were homosexual, it was the realization of, why are we being intimidated by a bunch of jerks who don't know anything about life? Who were they to tell us what to feel and how we're supposed to behave?

ALLEN GINSBERG
American poet, 1960s

Every person who commits any of the following acts shall be guilty of disorderly conduct, a misdemeanor: (a) Who solicits anyone to engage in or who in any public place or in any place open to the public or exposed to public view engages in lewd or dissolute conduct. . . . (d) Who loiters in or about any toilet open to the public for the purpose of engaging in or soliciting any lewd or lascivious or any unlawful act.

California Penal Code
Section 647, 1961

A case could be made, let us say, for removing criminal sanctions against homosexuality between consenting adults. But the modernists want to go further and, in effect, remove the moral sanctions against such behavior; and that is something else again. All that is good is not embodied in the law; and all that is evil is not proscribed by the law. A well-disciplined society needs few laws; but it needs strong mores.

WILLIAM F. BUCKLEY, JR.
American editor/author/television
personality, 1966

Oral copulation by and between two women constitutes "unnatural carnal copulation" within the statute proscribing such conduct.

Louisiana Supreme Court ruling, 1967

Sodomy (a legal term for anal intercourse) is a felony crime in most states, punishable by long prison terms. The name is derived from the Biblical city destroyed because of its "wickedness." But what were they doing in Gomorrah?

EUGENE SCHOENFELD, M.D.
American sexologist, 1968

Judges realize that putting a homosexual into prison is like trying to cure obesity by incarceration in a candy shop.

> MARTIN HOFFMAN
> American sexologist/psychologist, 1968

I'm all for bringing back the birch, but only between consenting adults.

> GORE VIDAL
> American writer, 1969

[On the police raiding of the Stonewall dance bar in Greenwich Village, June 27, 1969]

Cheers would go up as favorites would emerge from the door, strike a pose, and swish by the detective with a "Hello there, fella." The stars were in their element. Wrists were limp, hair was primped, and reactions to the applause were classic. "I gave them the gay power bit and they loved it, girls."

> *The Village Voice*, 1969

The gay lib movement should consolidate with the other lib movements—the women's lib movement, and particularly with the revolutionary movements which are nonviolent—and become a single thrust toward emancipation in America.

> TENNESSEE WILLIAMS
> American playwright, 1970s

The male party line concerning lesbians is that women became lesbians out of reaction to men. This is a pathetic illustration of the male ego's inflated proportions. I became a lesbian because of women, because women are beautiful, strong and compassionate. Secondarily, I became a lesbian because the culture that I live in is violently anti-woman.

RITA MAE BROWN
American writer, 1970

To love without role, without power plays, is revolution.

RITA MAE BROWN
American writer, 1970

Women-identified women will not sell out. Neither will we go around making loud noises about killing pigs and blowing up the Capitol. Talk is cheap, and violent talk is the cheapest of all. We are not taken in by the easy politics of violence just as we are not taken in by the more clever politics of reform. We have no instant formula that will dazzle reporters and media vultures. We have mountains to move, and we have, today, only our hands to move them with. But every day there are more hands.

RITA MAE BROWN
American writer, 1970

I think Anita Bryant was one of the best things that has happened for the cause of gay liberation. She forced even conservative gays to come out of their closets. But now self-criticism has to be pushed even further. No sentimental shit about gays as poor little victims.

ROSA VON PRAUNHEIM
German director/writer, 1971

We have to define for ourselves a new pluralistic, rolefree social structure. It must contain both the freedom and the physical space for people to live alone, live together for a while, live together for a long time, either as couples or in large numbers; and the ability to flow easily from one of these states to another as our needs change.

CARL WITTMAN
American writer/activist, 1972

We are the negation of heterosexuality and of the nuclear family structure, and as such we have been driven from our jobs, our families, our education, and sometimes from life itself.

KARLA JAY
American writer, 1972

A Lesbian is a woman whose primary erotic, psychological, emotional and social interest is in a member of her own sex, even though that interest may not be overtly expressed. . . . Like her heterosexual sister, the Lesbian has been downtrodden, but doubly so: first, because she is a woman, and second, because she is a Lesbian.

DEL MARTIN AND PHYLLIS LYON
American gay activists/writers, 1972

They kept us locked up for six months. For six months I went through every book in the library, I knitted doilies, I went through four bookkeeping courses. I was by myself in a cell maybe a yard wide and a yard deep. No toilets. We had a shit pail with disinfectant in it. We constructed our own toilet seats for our little pails, which we took out and emptied twice a day, then filled up with disinfectant again. They loved us so much they put the entire TB ward on the deck right below us, because it didn't make any difference if the homosexuals and sexual perverts got TB.

> Guy T. Olmstead
> American convict imprisoned for
> homosexual acts, 1973

The rights and dignity of homosexuals are not a controversial issue.

> Gay Activists Alliance and
> National Gay Task Force
> 1973

Homosexuality is a worldwide economic fact.

> William S. Burroughs
> American novelist, 1973

Bisexuality is not so much a copout as a fearful compromise.

> Jill Johnston
> American feminist/gay activist, 1973

Somebody was asking me. Said he thought Richard Nixon was obviously homosexual. I said: "Why do you think that?" He said: "You know, that funny, uncoordinated way he moves." I said: "Yeah, like Nureyev."

Gore Vidal
American writer, 1973

Women who practice bisexuality today are simply leading highly privileged lives that do not challenge male power and that, in fact, undermine the feminist struggle.

Loretta Ulmschreider
American writer/feminist, 1974

There's a lot of political and communal development open to the gay lib movement as it includes more and more varieties of love, besides genital, and it may be that the bridge between gay liberation and men's liberation may be in the mutual recognition of the masculine tenderness that was denied both groups for so long.

Allen Ginsberg
American poet, 1975

At first, I thought gay liberation would mean freedom from sexual bondage, leaving your mate, the women's liberation stuff that comics make fun of. Later, I discovered that the most important part was finding yourself.

Arthur Bell
American writer, 1977

It is the law that perverts sexual relationships. Law can only be changed by political action.

GORE VIDAL
American writer, 1977

I don't really believe in politics. Politics is the art of making the inevitable appear to be a matter of wise human choice. I don't think any of us need take it seriously in any way.

QUENTIN CRISP
English writer/critic, 1979

When I turn on my television, what does it show me? Someone stomping through the street screeching for equal pay—equal opportunity. Equal is a dead word. Never take as your object in life the desire to be anybody's equal. Once you have entered the profession of being, you have become a professor of a subject on which you are the only living authority. What other people do with their life, with their style, will not matter.

QUENTIN CRISP
English writer/critic, 1979

That [a self-proclaimed homosexual was named to the Criminal Court of New York City] says, as it should to young gay people, that they can be who they are, that they do not have to dissemble about what they are, and that they can also achieve whatever their abilities will allow them to do. . . . Over the past years, many people have congratulated me on what they thought was my courage in moving forward, and coming out and standing up for the person I really am. . . . Yet throughout it all, my mother, my father, my brother, and my life partner have supported me with understanding and love.

RICHARD C. FAILLA
American judge, 1980s

Demonstrations which define the homosexual as a unique minority defeat the very cause for which the homosexual strives—to be an integral part of society.

SHIRLEY WILLER
American activist, 1980s

As a minority, we homosexuals are therefore caught in a particularly vicious circle. On the one hand, the shame of belonging and the social punishment of acknowledgment are so great that pretense is almost universal; on the other hand, only a leadership that would acknowledge [us] would be able to break down the barriers of shame and resultant discrimination.

DONALD WEBSTER CORY
American writer, 1980s

The right wing needs these witch hunts. . . . They believe fags are going to break into the toilets and piss on lovely virgins.

GORE VIDAL
American writer, 1980s

I am suggesting that heterosexuality, like motherhood, needs to be recognized and studied as a political institution—even, or especially, by those individuals who feel they are, in their personal experience, the precursors of a new social relation between the sexes.

ADRIENNE RICH
American poet, 1980s

In 1948, I went to a gay party and we started talking about forming a "Bachelors for Wallace" [organization]. . . . We would have a plank, and educate people about who we were, about how we weren't bad people; we would end entrapment, and begin a whole new movement for the gay peoples. I was so excited, I went home and wrote it all up. When I called them the next day, they all said, "Forget it, honey"; it was the beer.

HARRY HAY
American pioneer activist/writer, 1980s

We always find ourselves in the position of having to play civil libertarian to a bunch of bigots who want their constitutional right to express their hatred of us.

RONALD GOLD
American journalist/gay activist, 1980

Lesbian and gay rights will continue to be eroded unless the silence that usually greets these actions is broken.

ELEANOR COOPER AND JIM LEVIN
Coalition for Lesbian and Gay Rights, 1981

Most feminists probably don't give a tiny damn about the sex that gay men have together as long as in their lives they actively oppose the oppression of all women.

SALLY M. GEARHART
American science-fiction writer, 1982

The core of feminism is choice. All women and men are to have the freedom to choose whatever kind of lives they wish in a feminist society. They will not be constrained by gender expectations to choose a career, a particular lifestyle, or only one kind of sexuality. It was this vision of freedom that attracted me to feminism in the first place. I was a lesbian before I was a feminist, and a fag hag before I was aware of either. Now I am a revolting fag hag. Seeing the situation in the feminist community has made me revolt and proclaim my complete lack of sympathy for this parody of feminism.

LINDA FRANKEL
American feminist/gay rights activist, 1982

As women and as lesbians we have learned to reclaim names like dyke, bitch, manhater, golddigger, shrew, harpy, whore, cunt, amazon; (even) lesbian, even *woman* had first to be reclaimed from a place of squeamishness.

MELANIE KAYE
American writer/feminist, 1982

The simple, obvious thing would have been to go to the senior prom with a girl. But that would have been a lie—a lie to myself, to the girl, and to all the other students. What I wanted to do was to take a male date.

[At seventeen he stood up to community and school authorities and won their permission to bring a male date to his high school prom.]

AARON FRICKE
American writer/activist, 1982

"When are you going to make your mother
  twice a grandma?"
No way. My womb, like my fist,
  is clenched against the world.

MARTHA SHELLEY
American activist/poet, 1982

To choose only other lesbians means to deny the centuries of mothers,
the centuries of slaves behind her, in their particular prisons, forming
their particular prides, leaving inside of the daughters a particular
way. But to choose your mother as well as other lesbians renders all
lesbians vulnerable to the attacks of men as the mothers transmit
them, to the softer ties of false safety, the smell of holiday cooking,
the access to the material world the mother woos with, bringing her
daughter back home to the dungeon.

ELANA DYKEWOMON
American writer/activist, 1982

I don't know anyone who has a lower opinion of the attitudes that
people have toward gay people than Harvey Milk had. He assumed
that the most liberal people in our society despise gay people. But
he always acted as though that were not true.

HARRY BRITT
American politician/clergyman, 1982

Homosexuals are usually too self-directed to turn toward politics.

NED ROREM
American composer, 1982

It is the same American mistake. To believe that having the same understanding, the same conclusion from the same facts, makes us therefore the same. It is anti-separatism to believe that in order to have a motion, it must all be the same motion, that all the words of the new language must come from the same root; it is mindless melting pot politics, to give away what has made you, to come forward pretending you are a blank slate.

ELANA DYKEWOMON
American writer/activist, 1982

There is less and less doubt that the women's movement is perfectly willing to bully gay men over issues of male sexual expression.

JOHN PRESTON
American writer, 1983

In 1834, Alabama Senator William Rufus De Vane King (a fifty-seven-year-old bachelor) met Pennsylvania Senator James Buchanan, and the two were inseparable until King's appointment as U.S. minister to France. Their intimate relationship caused barbed comments in Washington. Andrew Jackson called King "Miss Nancy." . . . Aaron Brown (in 1844, in a private letter) called King Buchanan's "better half," referred jestingly to King and Buchanan's "divorce," and referred to King as "she," "her," and "Aunt Fancy"; King refers to his "communion" with Buchanan in a note of 1844.

JONATHAN KATZ
American historian, 1983

[Quoted on the Quilt panel commemorating his death from AIDS]

I came here today to ask that this nation with all its resources and compassion not let my epitaph read he died of red tape.

ROGER LYON
American AIDS activist, 1983

One must again fall back on the fact that gay politics still rely on the dynamic of failure, still count on being rebuked as a means to mobilize the great unwashed apathetic folk who merely need the right incentive to get involved. Behind this is a fantasy that one day gays, charged by some apocalyptic defeat, will march by the millions, shoulder to shoulder, through the streets of the nation. It is time to point out that this has nothing to do with politics.

LARRY BUSH
American journalist, 1983

They call Ronald Reagan the great communicator. Well, any man that can call a nuclear missile "Peacemaker" is free to call his son "Butch."

TOM AMMIANO
American comedian, 1984

From the law's point of view the only weakness of the decoy system was that it took two constables to apprehend one sexual offender. This was a waste of manpower.

QUENTIN CRISP
English writer/critic, 1984

However low a man sinks he never reaches the level of the police.

QUENTIN CRISP
English writer/critic, 1984

If soliciting is a crime because it is a nuisance to those who do not wish to be importuned, then not only I but most homosexuals are guiltless. Very few men would dare to annoy strangers by detaining them against their will or even continuing to speak to them if the slightest irritation were evinced.

QUENTIN CRISP
English writer/critic, 1984

No matter which sex I went to bed with, I never smoked on the street.

FLORENCE KING
American writer, 1985

The first gay meeting which grew into the gay liberation movement was held in 1950 in someone's apartment in Los Angeles, and the door was locked and the blinds were drawn and there was a lookout posted because they thought it was illegal to talk about homosexuality.

BARBARA GITTINGS
American director of the Gay Task Force,
American Library Association, 1985

We have cooperated for a very long time in the maintenance of our own invisibility. And now the party is over.

VITO RUSSO
American film historian/writer, 1985

Don't make derisive remarks about the lesbians who are marching with you.

TONY LANG
American humorist, 1985

Homosexuality, a moral wrong, cannot be the basis of a civil right. Society doesn't make allowances for alcoholics, murderers, or rapists even if they are biologically predisposed to do what they do. Why should we have lower standards for homosexuals?

RABBI YEHUDA LEVIN
American religious leader, 1986

I have come to think that both sex and politics are a mistake and that any attempt to establish a connection between the two is the greatest error of all.

QUENTIN CRISP
English writer/critic, 1986

I didn't start the sexual liberation movement, but I was a part of it when it was ready to start.

CHRISTINE JORGENSEN
Pioneer American transsexual, 1927–1989

It was inevitable that outrageousness exploded with the beginnings of gay liberation. Hooray for sassy risk and silly experiment and anarchic joy!

JAMES BROUGHTON
American poet/playwright/filmmaker, 1987

I simply refuse to give up the party of Lincoln to the bigots. . . . I know that most Republicans don't have a very good track record on gay rights, but I believe that someday the Republican party will come around, absolutely. Otherwise, what's the alternative? To put all our eggs in one basket?

> LEONARD MATLOVICH
> American Air Force sergeant discharged for
> being gay, 1988

We hold that the Army's regulations violate the constitutional guarantee of equal protection of the laws because they discriminate against persons of homosexual orientation.

> Appeals Panel
> U.S. Court, 1988

Ironically, according to some estimates, as many as 20 to 25 percent of the officers in the San Francisco Police Department are gay men or lesbians.

> CHARLES LINEBARGER
> American journalist, 1988

[Comment to New York Senate Republicans regarding their reluctance to specifically include gay people in recent antibias legislation]

Are you playing God and judging that this group is morally wrong and should not be protected? And if you are making that judgment, why don't you stand up in public to the people of this state to see if they agree with you?

> MARIO CUOMO
> Governor of New York, 1988

It's a witch hunt. The Government is backing Section 28 because they think it's popular. The more people who can demonstrate we aren't as prejudiced as the Government thinks we are, the better.

London *Gay Times*, 1988

Rare are reports of straight people arrested in lovers' lanes, but gay men are frequently hauled in. Some undercover cops go to great lengths to entice gay men into taking the bait. Officers have been known to smile and wink and rub their groins. Their activity at times borders on entrapment.

DAVE WALTER
American journalist, 1988

[Comment regarding the police spying on gay groups in Massachusetts]

This just goes to prove my long-standing theory: Some straight men—or should I say semi-straight men or hoping-and-praying-they're-straight men—just can't seem to get enough of anything gay. They're fascinated. Entranced. Some would say obsessed. No excuse is too flimsy.

MARGERY EAGAN
American journalist, 1988

Sexual activities in places that are truly public are crimes and should legitimately be crimes.

TOM STODDARD
American activist/Lambda organizer, 1988

The pressures of growing up gay, developing a gay persona in a straight society, and then acclimating one's lifestyle comfortably into society makes a person particularly sensitive to undercurrents in social issues. Due to this cultural trait, the gay community will become an influential segment of the population and will be recognized as economically and politically powerful.

IAN LYNCH
American image consultant, 1988

I have a duty, and I intend to fulfill that duty, and my duty is to assist people who are gay or lesbian or who have AIDS to be free of discrimination. I will perform that duty, and I'm not going to look back to see how many people wished I had or wished I hadn't, because my clients are very happy that they have someone to assist them, and they are my main concern.

GLORIA ALLRED
American attorney/feminist, 1988

America is not a blanket, woven from one thread, one color, one cloth. [We] must build a quilt together. . . . Blacks and Hispanics, when we fight for civil rights, we are right—but our patch isn't big enough. Gays and lesbians, when you fight against discrimination and for a cure for AIDS, you are right—but your patch isn't big enough. Conservatives and progressives, when you fight for what you believe, you are right—but your patch isn't big enough. . . . But when we bring the patches together, we make a quilt. . . . [Then] we, the people, always win.

JESSE JACKSON
American politician, 1988

[Placard message from demonstrations in Holland during Queen Elizabeth II's state visit, following the institution of the new Section 28]

God Save the Queens.

Protest placard slogan, 1988

[Comment regarding the Democratic platform's unwillingness to mention gay rights issues]

Call us by name.

TERJE ANDERSON
American politician, 1988

The U.S. Olympics Committee singled out the Gay Olympics with a lawsuit prohibiting the use of the word "Olympics." They didn't sue the Armenian Olympics, the Black Olympics, the Chinese Olympics. They only sued the Gay Olympics. I know that the USOC claims that it was a question of trademark law, not homophobia. But let me tell you this: Anyone who believes that must think that Rosa Parks's struggle to sit where she wanted on a Montgomery bus was really about transit policy.

ART AGNOS
Mayor of San Francisco, 1988

[Note accompanying quilt panel to NAMES Project honoring Dr. Tom Waddell, Olympic decathlete and founder of the Gay "Olympics"]

Every stitch in Dr. Tom Waddell's quilt is a stitch of rage—for the insensitivity of the present administration to act against this epidemic, for the misunderstanding of some, but most of all to the United States Supreme Court for their denial of the use of the word "Olympic" associated with games Dr. Waddell founded.

Shame on you!

Shame on you, not only for the denial of the use of the word "Olympic," but also shame on you that my quilt for Dr. Thomas Waddell doesn't have love in every stitch.

A. CHRISTOPHER PRIESTLY
American activist, 1988

[We] have allowed our governors to divide the population into two teams. [One] is good, godly, straight; the other is evil, sick, vicious.

GORE VIDAL
American writer, 1988

Sure, I would fight for access to Tompkins Square Park. I've met some of my most gratifying sexual partners there. In fact I've *had* some of my most gratifying sexual experiences there.

CLIFFORD SCHWARTZ
American journalist, 1988

[Addressing the Democratic National Convention]

I am frustrated with those who call me a victim, stripping me of both my personal and political power. I am not a victim. I cannot think of myself as a victim and survive. I am a person with AIDS.

KEITH GANN
American politician, 1988

PSYCHOLOGY

In theory, at least, psychology is a science and is therefore neutral; its only purpose is to discover the nature of the soul. In practice, however, psychology is a horrible thing to happen to anybody. In the 1920s and '30s, when it was ludicrously fashionable, everyone with sufficient leisure read books by people like Freud and felt that this gave them a secret superiority over others. Their strategy consisted of asking their friends why they did something for which the motive was, in fact, self-evident and, upon receiving a simple answer, saying with a smirk, "But that's only your conscious reason."

Irritating though this behavior was, it was really only a parlor game.

Psychotherapy, as opposed to mere psychological games, is much more pernicious. It is a fiendish and expensive way of tampering with the lives of patients weak enough or foolish enough to seek outside help with personal problems for which, in fact, only will power is any solution.

Driven by God or their parents or, worse, their social workers, many homosexual men and women have sought the advice of psychotherapists. This is fatal. Instead of trying to persuade their patients that they must accept their differences from other people, that they must relinquish their grasp on family life and social acceptance and, instead, should concentrate on arming themselves against the hostilities of the world, these *witch doctors try to reshape the psyches of their victims so that they may take their place in society.*

What's so hot about society that anyone who does not know how should take his place in it?

What outsiders of any kind ought to do is to stay right where they are and wait for society to form itself round them.

It is only too obvious that if help for civilization is ever to arrive, it will come not from the hands of those who, against all their instincts, have adapted themselves to the status quo but from those who by silent example have shown the world how to be more tolerant.

[The homosexual] disposition occurs in some people naturally. . . . When nature is responsible, no one would call such persons immoral, any more than they would women because they are passive in intercourse rather than active. . . . And whether the individual so disposed conquers or yields to it is not properly a moral issue.

ARISTOTLE
Greek philosopher/scientist
384 B.C.–322 B.C.

It certainly does not seem impossible to suppose that as the ordinary love has a special function in the propagation of the race, so the other has its special function in social and heroic work and in the generation not of bodily children but of those children of the mind—the philosophical conceptions and ideals which transform our lives and those of society.

EDWARD CARPENTER
English writer/activist, 1844–1929

Indulgent male inverts like pleasant, artistic things, and nearly all of them are fond of music. They also like praise and admiration. They are poor whistlers. Their favorite color is green. . . . Active male homosexuals are not prone to make sacrifices, personal or social, as was observed in the analysis of war neuroses. Some aggressive homosexual women wear male attire, and are often very proficient in business, sports, etc. The passive ones are of the clinging type, who like to kiss other girls.

JOHN F. W. MEAGHER
American psychiatrist, 1929

Every impulse that we strive to strangle broods in the mind and poisons us.

> OSCAR WILDE
> Irish writer, 1854–1900

It has been said that the great events of the world take place in the brain. It is in the brain, and the brain only, that the great sins of the world take place.

> OSCAR WILDE
> Irish writer, 1854–1900
> From *The Picture of Dorian Gray*

C. F. GILL, prosecutor at Wilde's second trial: I wish to call your attention to the style of your correspondence with Lord Alfred Douglas.

OSCAR WILDE: I am ready. I am never ashamed of the style of my writings.

GILL: Do you think an ordinarily constituted being would address such expressions to a younger man?

OSCAR WILDE: I am not, happily I think, an ordinarily constituted being.

> OSCAR WILDE
> Irish writer, 1854–1900
> From the transcript of his second trial

It is a great pity, in a way, that [Oscar] Wilde happened to have been born thirty or forty years too soon. Were he alive today, and were he willing to co-operate toward the relief or the removal of his endocrine unbalance, it is more than likely that a great deal might have been done for this erratic genius.

We could have subjected the overactive thymus to X-ray radiation, atrophied the gland and suppressed the overactivity of its function— which was one of the principal causes of Wilde's lack of sexual normality. . . .

We could also have given Wilde the benefit of an informed psychologic and psycho-analytic concept—the proper understanding of which might have worked wonders in his brilliant brain.

LA FOREST POTTER
American psychoanalyst, 1933

Homosexuality is assuredly no advantage, but it is nothing to be ashamed of, no vice, no degradation, it cannot be classified as an illness.

SIGMUND FREUD
Austrian neurologist/founder of
psychoanalysis, 1856–1939

Psycho-analysis has a common basis with biology, in that it presupposes an original bisexuality of human beings (as of animals).

SIGMUND FREUD
Austrian neurologist/founder of
psychoanalysis, 1856–1939

The removal of genital inversion, or homosexuality, is in my experience never an easy matter. I have rather found that success is possible only under specially favorable circumstances, and even then that it essentially consists in being able to open to the restricted homosexuals the way to the opposite sex, till then barred, thus restoring their full bisexual functions.

SIGMUND FREUD
Austrian neurologist/founder of
psychoanalysis, 1856–1939

Inversion [homosexuality] is found in people who exhibit no other serious deviations from the normal. It is similarly found in people whose efficiency is unimpaired, and who are indeed distinguished by specially high intellectual development and ethical culture.

SIGMUND FREUD
Austrian neurologist/founder of
psychoanalysis, 1856–1939

Psychoanalytic research very strongly opposes the attempt to separate homosexuals from other persons as a group of a special nature.

SIGMUND FREUD
Austrian neurologist/founder of
psychoanalysis, 1856–1939

The majority of homosexuals, male and female, are not degenerates.
. . . There are many persons who indulge in unnatural sexual relations
who are not homosexuals. They are the real degenerates. There are
many potential and active homosexuals whose intercourse with persons of their own sex is confined to emotional and intellectual contact,
to establishing romantic friendship. . . . There are others in which
intercourse is physical as well. The rank and file considers them
degenerates.

> JOSEPH COLLINS
> American neurologist, 1866–1950

All persons originally are bisexual in their predisposition. There are
no exceptions.

> WILHELM STEKEL
> Austrian psychiatrist/coworker of Freud's
> 1868–1940

The meeting of two personalities is like the contact of two chemical
substances: if there is any reaction, both are transformed.

> CARL GUSTAV JUNG
> Swiss psychiatrist/pioneer psychoanalyst
> 1875–1961

It is not enough to repeat that Shakespeare and Michael Angelo and
Alexander the Great and Rosa Bonheur and Sappho were intermedi-
ates: how is this science of the future to meet these issues?

> MARGARET ANDERSON
> American editor, 1886–1973

To be "cured" against one's will and cured of states which we may not regard as disease is to be put on a level with those who have not yet reached the age of reason.

C. S. Lewis
English scholar/writer, 1898–1963

I did not want them to start getting rough, so I said, pacifically, "Dear sweet clodhoppers, if you knew anything of sexual psychology you would know that nothing could give me keener pleasure than to be manhandled by you meaty boys. It would be an ecstasy of the very naughtiest kind. So if any of you wishes to be my partner in joy come and seize me. If, on the other hand, you simply wish to satisfy some obscure and less easily classified libido and see me bathe, come with me quietly, dear louts, to the fountain."

Evelyn Waugh
English writer, 1903–1966
Anthony Blanche, from *Brideshead Revisited*

When one is pretending, the entire body revolts.

Anaïs Nin
American writer, 1903–1977

The homosexual is often a man of considerable intellect and ability. It is found that the cycle of these individuals' homosexual desires follows the cycle closely patterned to the menstrual period of women. There may be three or four days in each month that the homosexual's instincts break down and drive the individual into abnormal fields of sexual practice. Under large doses of sedatives during this sensitive cycle, he may escape such acts.

Arthur Lewis Miller
U.S. Congressman, 1950

Homosexuality as a clinical entity does not exist. Its forms are as varied as are those of heterosexuality.

EVELYN HOOKER
American psychologist, 1957

There seems to be no valid evidence to show that homosexuality, per se, is a sickness. In view of the absence of such valid evidence, the simple fact that the suggestion of sickness has been made is no reason for entertaining it seriously, or for abandoning the view that homosexuality is not a sickness, but merely a liking or preference similar to and fully on a par with heterosexuality. Accordingly, I take the position unequivocally that, until and unless valid, positive evidence shows otherwise, homosexuality, per se, is neither a sickness, a defect, a disturbance, a neurosis, a psychosis, nor a malfunction of any sort.

FRANK KAMENY
American activist/founder of Washington
Mattachine Society, 1965

Virtually all the literature on homosexuality is marred by the failure of its authors to take account of the fact that heterosexuality is just as much a problematic situation for the student of human behavior as is homosexuality. The only reason it does not seem to us a problem is because we take its existence for granted.

MARTIN HOFFMAN
American sociologist, 1968

There is no definition of "homosexual" or "homosexuality" which is going to be agreed to by 100 percent of the scientists working in this field.

MARTIN HOFFMAN
American sociologist, 1968

Bachelor baboons who have restricted opportunities for contact with females sometimes strike up homosexual friendships, and for a time a masculine pair remains constantly together. Immature males often join full-grown bachelors and engage in sexual activity. Prepuberal and adolescent males show a wide range of sex responses. They display the feminine sexual presentation, masturbate, and mount one another. They also mount and are mounted by adult members of their own sex. And they engage in manual, oral, and olfactory genital examination with other males of their own age.

C. S. FORD AND F. A. BEACH
American sexologists, 1970

The branch of medicine we are most concerned with is psychiatry. The American medical profession is oblivious to the needs of oppressed people, and psychiatrists are clearly hostile to homosexuality.

CHICAGO GAY LIBERATION FOR
THE REVOLUTIONARY PEOPLE'S
CONSTITUTIONAL CONVENTION
Working Paper, 1970

I conceive of two distinct categories—heterosexual and homosexual. . . . The two categories are . . . mutually exclusive and cannot be placed on the same continuum. . . . A man is homosexual if his behavior is homosexual. Self-identification is not relevant.

IRVING BIEBER
American sexologist, 1971

You ask about what we were interested in finding out about homosexuality. Nothing vastly different than what we're looking for in heterosexuality. What makes it happen? I think when you find the answer to one, you find the answer to the other.

> VIRGINIA JOHNSON
> American sexologist, 1972

Homosexuality doesn't change people's basic traits. Especially their need to be wanted and loved.

> DAVID REUBEN
> Psychiatrist/author, 1972

Homosexuality—like heterosexuality—becomes self-fulfilling.

> PEPPER SCHWARTZ AND
> PHILIP BLUMSTEIN
> American sexologists, 1973

[My grandmother] had just begun practicing on her own, under Freud's supervision, in Vienna, and she took on a patient who was a Lesbian. My grandmother was disturbed because, although the analysis finally concluded successfully—the woman could deal with various problems in her life—she was still a Lesbian. My grandmother was rather worried about what Freud would say about this turn of events. When she next saw Freud the first thing he said was, "Congratulations on your great success with Miss X." My grandmother, startled, said, "But she's still a Lesbian." To which Freud replied, "What does it matter as long as she's happy?"

> NICHOLAS DEUTSCH
> Gay activist and grandson of
> Helene Deutsch, psychoanalyst, 1974

Admittedly homosexuals can be conditioned to react sexually to a woman, or to an old boot for that matter. In fact both homo- and heterosexual experimental subjects *have been* conditioned to react sexually to a boot—to an old boot. You can save a lot of money that way.

> WILLIAM S. BURROUGHS
> American novelist, 1978

The game [football] is a way of allowing us to have physical contact with other men. . . . The truth hurts, and I think I've struck a nerve. Face it, there's got to be more to football than a nice way to spend Saturday afternoon. Eighty thousand people don't turn out for the Roller Derby.

> ALAN DUNDES
> American psychiatrist, 1978

Homosexuality cannot be classed as a perversion on phenomenological grounds. Nothing rules out the full range of interpersonal perceptions between persons of the same sex.

> THOMAS NAGEL
> American philosopher, 1979

Nathan entered a Baptist college to study for the ministry. During that time he divulged to a minister at the college that he had had gay sex. Nathan was told to report to the health service doctor, who asked him to draw a picture of a person. Nathan drew a woman with an evening gown, a grand piano, and a circular staircase. The psychiatrist said, "You're an incurable homosexual." Nathan was asked no further questions, the fact was reported to the dean, and Nathan was expelled. He was placed in a hospital and aversion therapy was planned, but he refused it.

CHARLES SILVERSTEIN
American writer, 1981

It's hard for young people today to imagine that as little as 20 years ago a hundred gay people were sitting around arguing over whether or not they should say that they weren't mentally ill.

CRAIG RODWELL
American merchant/opened America's first
gay bookstore, 1982

Since many sex therapy techniques include the use of either commercial or educational erotica, it is problematic, although not surprising, that many lesbian clients find such male-created images either degrading or uninteresting.

LAURA S. BROWN
American psychologist/sexologist, 1986

RELIGION

I was once invited to address all the gay Catholics in America. Out of politeness, at the meeting I did not mention You-Know-Who, but on the way there I met one of the members of the group. I asked him if I might discuss with him certain religious matters and he gave me permission to do so.

We were in agreement that Jesus of Nazareth said almost nothing about sex and that his utterances form only the vaguest outline for a moral way of life. We also agreed that since his death the Church has inevitably become institutionalized and that the original public relations officer for the entire movement was St. Paul.

> ME: But Saint Paul didn't like sex of any kind—let alone kinky sex.
> HIM: True.
> ME: He wanted us to be made eunuchs for the kingdom of Heaven's sake. If we couldn't manage that, he grudgingly gave his permission for us to marry, but saying that it is better to marry than to burn is scarcely a hearty recommendation.
> HIM: No, but we are going to shift the emphasis from the teachings of Saint Paul to the sayings of Jesus of Nazareth.
> ME: And then you are going to convince your local bishops?
> HIM: Yes.
> ME: And then you are going to convince His Holiness?
> HIM: Yes.

This seemed to me then and still seems an unrealistic program. I am not a theologian and it is not for me to say whether or not the pope is infallible, but of one thing I am certain: he is unbudgeable. It is when civilization is crumbling that people turn to the Church. If it is in a perpetual state of flux, what use would it be?

Why, if any gay person is of a religious disposition, does he not choose a different faith? I have been informed that there is a Far Eastern creed whose male members are enjoined to engage in homosexual intercourse at least once in a lifetime, because when the new messiah arrives on earth, he will have two fathers and no mother.

Zeus, to steal boy Ganymede,
　An eagle's form put on;
And when he wanted the lady Leda
　He turned into a swan.

Now some like girls, and some like boys;
　But the moral's plain to see:
If both are good enough for Zeus,
　They're good enough for me.

> ANONYMOUS
> Greek poet

Those very people who have been nourished by godly doctrine, who instruct others in what they ought and ought not to do, who have heard the Scriptures brought down from heaven, these do not consort with prostitutes as fearlessly as they do with young men.

The fathers of the young men take this in silence: they do not try to sequester their sons, nor do they seek any remedy for this evil.

None is ashamed, no one blushes, but, rather, they take pride in their little game; the chaste seem to be the odd ones, and the disapproving the ones in error.

> ST. JOHN CHRYSOSTOM
> Bishop of Constantinople, 347–407

Scorch, God, with a blow of your thunderbolt, the enemy of nature Who wastes the labor of creation in the lap of a male.

> ANONYMOUS
> Medieval monk, 1150?

I dwelt amonge the Sodomytes,
The Beniamytes, and Madyanytes,
And nowe the popysshe hypocrytes
Embrace me every where.

JOHN BALE
English bishop/author, 1495–1563
Sodomismus, allegorical monk in a satirical
anti-Catholic poem

St. John the Evangelist was bedfellow to Christ.

CHRISTOPHER MARLOWE
English poet/playwright, 1564–1593

The Lord of Heaven send you a sweet and blithe awakening, all kind
of comfort in your sanctified bed, and bless the fruits thereof, that
I may have sweet Bedchamber boys to play with me (and this is my
daily prayer).

KING JAMES I
King of Scotland and Great Britain
1566–1625

If it be sin to love a lovely lad, oh, then sin I.

RICHARD BARNFIELD
English poet, 1574–1627

Come, my Lucasia, since we see
  That Miracles Men's faith do move,
By wonder and by prodigy
  To the dull angry world let's prove
There's a Religion in our Love.

> KATHERINE PHILIPS
> English poet, 1631–1664

No David could woo his Jonathan more
Than our hearts have wooed each other.
How sweet 't would be, as true souls' friends,
To strive for the dearest blessing of all
From God, the greatest of all Friends.

[From a poem to her friend, Maria Bavink]

> AAGJE DEKEN
> Dutch poet/novelist, 1741–1804

Jesus has on the whole field of sexual irregularity preserved an uninterrupted silence.

> JEREMY BENTHAM
> English jurist/philosopher, 1748–1832
> From "Nonconformity"

It is so true that a woman may be in love with a woman, and a man with a man. It is pleasant to be sure of it, because it is undoubtedly the same love that we shall feel when we are angels, when we ascend to the only fit place for the Mignons, where *sie fragen nicht nach Mann und Weib* ["they do not ask about man or woman"].

> MARGARET FULLER
> American critic/social reformer, 1810–1850

Divine am I, inside and out, and I make holy whatever I touch or am
    touch'd from,
The scent of these arm-pits aroma finer than prayer,
The head more than churches, bibles and all creeds.
If I worship one thing more than another it shall be the spread of
    my body, or any part of it,
Translucent mould of me it shall be you! . . .
I dote on myself, there is that lot of me and all so luscious.

> WALT WHITMAN
> American poet, 1819–1892

What is called good is
perfect, and what is
called sin is just as
perfect.

> WALT WHITMAN
> American poet, 1819–1892

We are punished for our refusals. The body sins once, and has done
with its sin. The only way to get rid of a temptation is to yield to it.

> OSCAR WILDE
> Irish writer, 1854–1900

They do not sin at all
Who sin for love.

> OSCAR WILDE
> Irish writer, 1854–1900
> From "The Duchess of Padua"

I sought by love alone to go
Where God had writ an awful No;
Pride gave a guilty God to hell:
I have no pride: by love I fell.

Why this was done I cannot tell,
The mystery is inscrutable:
I only know I pay the cost
With heart and soul and honor lost.

> SIR ROGER CASEMENT
> Irish politician/social reformer, 1864–1916

Is it too much to ask that I should be
   Allowed to prove
God's gift of infinite variety
   In human love?

> JOHN BARFORD
> English poet, 1886–1935
> From "Toleration"

Oh happy John! Such love can never end.
Closer than brothers are is friend to friend.
   You the divinity of it have proved,
   "Whom Jesus loved."

> JOHN BARFORD
> English poet, 1886–1935
> From "Toleration"

Acknowledge us, oh God, before the whole world. Give us also the right to our existence!

> RADCLYFFE HALL
> English novelist, 1886–1943
> Stephen Gordon, in *The Well of Loneliness*

Wystan [W. H. Auden] doesn't love God, he's just attracted to him.

> MARC BLITZSTEIN
> American composer/author, 1905–1964

[Tennessee Williams] was—and is—guilt-ridden, and although he tells us that he believes in no afterlife, he is still too much the puritan not to believe in sin. At some deep level Tennessee truly believes that the homosexualist is wrong and that the heterosexualist is right.

> GORE VIDAL
> American writer, 1945

A turkish bath, like the Quaker service, is a place of silent meeting. The silence is shared solely by men, men who come uniquely together not to speak but to act.

> NED ROREM
> American composer, 1967

I live no longer in the usual world. I have forsaken the familiar. And soon, by an extreme gesture, I shall cease altogether to be human and become legend like Jesus, Buddha, Cybele.

> GORE VIDAL
> American writer, 1968
> Myra Breckinridge, in *Myra Breckinridge*

Did you hear about the gay choirboy who choked on his first hymn?

> American joke, 1970s

How can you tell if you walk into a gay church?

Only half the congregation is kneeling.

American joke, 1970s

[Jesus Christ] never married, ran around with twelve guys, and was even betrayed by a kiss from another guy.

THE REVEREND TROY PERRY
American clergyman/gay religious rights
activist, 1972

The Lord Is My Shepherd and He Knows I'm Gay.
[The title of his autobiography]

THE REVEREND TROY PERRY
American clergyman/gay religious rights
activist, 1977

I'm perfectly willing to accept the gay churches as a tactic. It may be a good idea to get in with the Jesus Christers. When you run with the wolves, said St. Lenin (Eastern rite orthodox), you must howl with the wolves.

GORE VIDAL
American writer, 1977

Platonic friendships in ancient Athens were hardly chaste. Sexual experiences, even orgies, were supposed to bring about catharsis and purgation to both body and soul—the embrace of a male prostitute and a pretty boy led to salvation!

ROBERT BRAIN
American writer, 1977

The Argentinians believed in Mrs. Perón. So much so, that when she died, they petitioned the pope to make her a saint. His Holiness declined. But if he'd consented, what a triumph for style that would have been. A double fox stole, ankle-strapped shoes, and eternal life. Nobody's ever had that.

QUENTIN CRISP
English writer/critic, 1979

I am unable to believe in a God susceptible to prayer. I simply haven't the nerve to imagine a being, a force, a cause which keeps the planets revolving in their orbits, and then suddenly stops in order to give me a bicycle with three speeds.

QUENTIN CRISP
English writer/critic, 1979

All cults are a mistake.

QUENTIN CRISP
English writer/critic, 1979

The range of behavior among those with a homosexual orientation is the same as among heterosexuals. Much homosexual behavior is sinful, but not simply by the fact that it is homosexual.

BISHOP MELVIN WHEATLEY
American religious leader/spokesman for gay rights, 1980s

Do you feel it's right for priests to get married?

Only if they're in love.

American joke, 1980s

Our ministry is one of public manifestation and habitual penetration. Our motto is "Give up the guilt." And we're going to do that through any form at our means—theater, dance, spiritual expression and therapy.

Sisters of Perpetual
Indulgence
American performance group, 1981

The condemnation of sex is not the basis of the conflict between primitive religious groups and homosexuality. The fundamentalists insist that all members of the religious community subordinate their personal feelings and goals to those of the group—individuals share the love of Jesus, and the rules for loving are laid down by the church elders. Homosexuality respects individual rights and identifies with personal goals. Therefore, being gay is not only a violation of theology (as fundamentalists see it), but an attack on the power of social control in the community.

Charles Silverstein
American writer, 1981

Sexual union is the most religious experience possible, it is the most thrilling form of meditation, it is direct contact with the divine.

James Broughton
American poet/playwright/filmmaker, 1982

According to Jewish Law, [lesbians] do not exist. I assure you, it's all very logical: we're not proscribed because we don't exist. If we existed, believe me, they'd be against us.

Evelyn Torton Beck
American writer/activist/professor, 1982

In spite of my experience, I wouldn't say the convent is a hotbed of lesbianism. I think that many women have joined convents to escape sexuality, whether lesbian or heterosexual. A desire for obedience and dedication to God are often secondary to a need for celibacy and denial. The convent appears to be a haven, a world apart from the pressures and risks of this world. But such shelter exacts a price in self-denial that I was unwilling to pay. I wanted to affect this world, not remove myself from it.

JEAN O'LEARY
Former nun, 1984

I am not saying that it is impossible to be a gay religious: I am saying that for me it was not possible. I could not keep the two worlds apart. I wanted to be part of the lesbian community, and I also wanted the awe and respect that "Sister" evokes in the Catholic community. Not being true to either world was causing havoc within me. For me the bottom line was celibacy. Although I am more celibate now than I was in the convent, I am free to choose it, and that makes all the difference.

CHARLOTTE DOCLAR
Former nun, 1984

My belief in a creator gave me my key; for as his creation, my desires and needs can be perceived as natural. Thus I live honestly as a gay person.

BENJAMIN MARCUS
American theologian, 1984

Christians cannot allow homosexuals to have any more power or strength in this country.

CHRISTIANS FOR REAGAN
Television advertisement, 1984

To be suddenly in a church where lesbians and gay men are accepted is an overwhelming experience. You're surprised to find those others because you thought you were the only gay Christian in the world.

KAREN ZIEGLER
Protestant minister, 1985

Homosexuals are the nicest people you can ever meet. They're kind, they're artistic, they are lonely people. You can't hate 'em to Jesus, you got to love 'em to Jesus.

LITTLE RICHARD
American rock performer/preacher, 1985

When I came out as a Lesbian, I traced my roots to Lesbos, claiming the Greek and Roman Goddesses as my own. Now I pray to darker Goddesses—Asherah, Mahalath, Amaterasu—whose names fill my mouth with joy.

SAPPHIRE
American activist, 1985

The bible-thumpers complain that erotica is to be blamed for nearly all of the sexual crimes in existence. Poppycock. Nothing could be farther from the truth. After a reader of gay male erotica becomes aroused, chances are minimal that he'll go out looking for sex on the streets.

SAMUEL M. STEWARD
American writer, 1985

There is no relationship more curious than the one that exists between gay people and organized religion, for they have long been
among its greatest sufferers and saints.

MARK THOMPSON
American writer, 1987

The church remains today as closeted a community as any other
major social institution, but with an unusually high proportion of
homosexuals. Some sources within the church say that at least a third,
if not more, of the hierarchy and clergy are gay.

MALCOLM BOYD
American Episcopal priest/poet/author
1987

The Holy Male is potential in every one of us. Men should be shown
how to reach and to cherish the divine in one another. A quest for
the ecstatic goes beyond cruising for a congenial sex object. It is not
enough to get it up, get it on, and get it over with. In the urgency
of our present situation we should look toward connecting imagina-
tively with the souls of our brothers.

JAMES BROUGHTON
American poet/playwright/filmmaker, 1987

Whereas heteros believe that spirituality requires the fervent denial
of carnality . . . for us gay folk the preprogrammed instinctual
behaviors triggered by, and thus awakened by, our early sexual and
sensual discoveries constitute for us the gateway to the growth of
spirit in heart and mind.

HARRY HAY
American writer/activist, 1987

I wouldn't recommend [that] a gay person join the Lutheran Church. I don't think it's possible for a gay person with integrity to stay within the church and not expect to fight.

JEFF JOHNSON
American Lutheran seminarian, 1988

If there's a heaven, there they live.
    Our hell is at their side,
for, if they blame or, worse, forgive,
    where shall we hide?

QUENTIN CRISP
English writer/critic, 1988

[Comment regarding the controversial opening of a home for people with AIDS in San Francisco proposed by Mother Teresa's Roman Catholic order]

You have nothing to fear. The sisters will bring with them a special grace, and everyone will feel better for the work they do. Dying is not something to be ashamed of or hidden away.

EDMUND G. BROWN, JR.
Former Governor of California, 1988

There is a light in this world, a healing spirit more powerful than any darkness we may encounter. We sometimes lose sight of this force when there is suffering, too much pain. Then suddenly, the spirit will emerge through the lives of ordinary people who hear a call and answer in extraordinary ways.

MOTHER TERESA
Religious leader/humanitarian, 1980s

SEPARATION AND LONELINESS

A person is lonely only if he does not know what to do with the time he spends by himself. The unnatural terror of being alone is entirely the result of family training. Parents who have endured the degradation of communal living see no reason why their children should escape its horrors. They therefore teach them to fear being alone—to regard singleness as a disgrace. Every sign of oddity observed in a child is a pretext for saying, "If you carry on like that, you'll end up alone." A long, dark time has to elapse before the infant learns to say, "Thank Heavens for that."

It is possible that because homosexual men and women realize that they live on the outermost fringe of family life and of society, they fear loneliness more than other people. They used to deal with this dread by being sociable to the edge of hysteria. A hostess could rely on this. She said to her husband, "I've made a list of our friends for the party; now we need a couple of queers who will waltz round the room distributing plates and pleasantries." These antics are no longer acceptable to the gay community; they now deal with the threat of loneliness by grouping together in uneasy comradeship, like an embattled military unit.

Because outsiders tend to gravitate to big cities, in a superficial sense homosexual men and women seldom experience loneliness; they can always go to a gay bar or a gay restaurant or a gay party, but there *are people who, donning enigmatic expressions, state that it is possible to be lonely in a crowd.*

One of the situations in which everybody seems to fear loneliness is death. In tones drenched with pity, people say of someone, "He died alone." I have never understood this point of view. Who wants to have to die and be polite at the same time?

For me, the vernal garlands bloom no more.
  Adieu! fond hope of mutual fire
With boy or girl in still-renewed desire!

> HORACE
> Roman poet/satirist, 65 B.C.–8 B.C.

I wonder and cannot express my amazement
That my John has not hurried back to me,
Though he is forever promising that he will return.
Either the boy is sick, or he has forgotten me. . . . The boy is
fickle like everything young.

> BAUDRI OF BOURGUEIL
> French Benedictine abbot/poet, 1046–1130

Sometimes I wish that I his pillow were,
So I might steale a kisse.

> RICHARD BARNFIELD
> English poet, 1574–1627

[Letter from Bologna after his banishment from England for gay affairs]

I am sure my Bones would not rest in an English grave—or my Clay
mix with the earth of that Country:—I believe the thought would
drive me mad on my death-bed could I suppose that any of my friends
would be base enough to convey my carcase back to your soil—I
would not even feed your worms—if I could help it.

> LORD BYRON
> English poet, 1788–1824

Is there even one other like me—distracted, his
    friend, his lover, lost to him?

                WALT WHITMAN
                American poet, 1819–1892

      For he, the one I cannot content myself
   Without—soon I saw him content himself without me,
Hours when I am forgotten—(O weeks and months are passing, but
   I
believe I am never to forget!)
Sullen and suffering hours—(I am ashamed—but
    it is useless—*I am what I am;*)

                WALT WHITMAN
                American poet, 1819–1892

But merely of two simple men I saw today on the pier
    in the midst of the crowd, parting the parting of dear friends,
The one to remain hung on the other's neck and
        passionately kissed him,
While the one to depart tightly pressed the one
    to remain in his arms.

                WALT WHITMAN
                American poet, 1819–1892

Now of all that city I remember only the man who wandered with me
there, for love of me. Day by day, and night by night, we were
together. All else has long been forgotten by me—I remember, I say,
only one rude and ignorant man, who, when I departed, long and long
held me by the hand with silent lips, sad and tremulous.

                WALT WHITMAN
                American poet, 1819–1892

[Comments regarding his friend, Peter Doyle]

Where are you, Pete? Oh! I'm feeling rather kinky—not at all peart,
Pete—not at all.

> WALT WHITMAN
> American poet, 1819–1892

Yet each man kills the thing he loves,
    By each let this be heard,
Some do it with a bitter look,
    Some with a flattering word,
The coward does it with a kiss,
    The brave man with a sword.

> OSCAR WILDE
> Irish writer, 1854–1900

And alien tears will fill for him
Pity's long-broken urn,
For his mourners will be outcast men,
And outcasts always mourn.

[Epitaph on Oscar Wilde's tomb: lines from his "The Ballad of Reading Gaol"]

> OSCAR WILDE
> Irish writer, 1854–1900

I weep these three dead: You the most regretted; and he who re-
sponded with a touching love, the other who, without dying, deserted
me, whose name sometimes comes back to me like a song.

> COMTE ROBERT DE MONTESQUIEU
> French poet/essayist, 1855–1921

The disappearance of a strong father in childhood not infrequently favors the inversion [homosexuality].

SIGMUND FREUD
Austrian neurologist/founder of
psychoanalysis, 1856–1939

He's lost him completely, as though he never existed.
Through fantasy, through hallucination,
he tries to find his lips in the lips of other young men,
he longs to feel his kind of love once more.

CONSTANTINE P. CAVAFY
Greek poet/linguist, 1863–1933

[Comment regarding her motive for murdering Freda Ward, 1892]

I killed Freda because I loved her, and she refused to marry me. I asked her three times to marry me, and at last she consented. We were to marry here and go to St. Louis to live. I sent her an engagement ring and she wore it for a time. When she returned it I resolved to kill her. I would rather she were dead than separated from me living.

ALICE MITCHELL
American society girl/murderess, 1892

[To her schoolteacher Fräulein von Bernberg]

I don't know how to say it . . . but . . . every time you say goodnight to me, and then go away, and shut the door of your room, I feel so terribly lost. . . . I stare at your door through the darkness . . . I keep on staring and staring . . . and I long to get up . . . open your door, creep up to your bed, and kneel beside it. I want to take your hand, and . . . and tell you . . . but I know I mustn't, so I have to clutch hard to my bed—I grip it so tight that it hurts. . . . Oh, I love you!

> CHRISTA WINSLOE
> German playwright, 1932
> Manuela, in *Girls in Uniform*

There can be no relation more strange, more critical, than that between two beings who know each other only with their eyes, who meet daily, yes, even hourly, eye each other with a fixed regard, and yet by some whim or freak of convention feel constrained to act like strangers.

> THOMAS MANN
> German novelist, 1875–1955
> Narrator, in *Death in Venice*

He would not—and this was the test—pretend to care about women when the only sex that attracted him was his own. He loved men and always had loved them. He longed to embrace them and mingle his being with theirs. Now that the man who returned his love had been lost, he admitted this.

> E. M. FORSTER
> English author, 1879–1970
> Narrator, in *Maurice*

[From a letter to her sister, Vanessa Bell]

You will never succumb to the charms of any of your sex— What an arid garden the world must be for you.

VIRGINIA WOOLF
English novelist, 1882–1941

I do not like to sleep at night, with your head against my shoulder; for I think of death, which comes so soon and enfolds us in too much sleep. I shall die, you will live: that is what keeps me awake. And yet another fear: one day not to hear you breathing and your heart beating beside me.

JEAN COCTEAU
French writer/director, 1889–1963

Let our hearts break provided they break together.

C. S. LEWIS
British scholar/writer, 1898–1963

I think that for the moment the homosexual minority is obliged to remain rather isolated, to be a group in this prudish society, a group which is separated from it and which cannot blend into this society. I think that it should reject this society and, to a certain extent, hate it. Homosexuals should reject this society, but the only thing that they can hope for at present in certain countries is a kind of free space, where they can come together among themselves, as in the United States, for example.

JEAN-PAUL SARTRE
French philosopher/novelist/dramatist/critic
1905–1980

[Last words of Truman Capote when asked by friend Joanne Carson, "Are you all right?"]

No, I'm not. But I soon will be.

TRUMAN CAPOTE
American writer, 1924–1984

The bachelor, simply because he's used to it, will confront oncoming solitude with more felicity and circumspection than the widower. Now the confirmed bachelor is probably pederastical, since the sexuality of ninety-nine out of one hundred unmarried men over forty is suspect, and the one hundredth is no Casanova but a hermit. Of course it doesn't follow that a homosexual is more circumspect and felicitous than a hetero (we know better), but then again it's not sure he's *less* so. But he *is* more versed in loneliness, thanks to his dubious talent for promiscuity.

NED ROREM
American composer, 1967

How much of all this did I enjoy, this long pursuit of love through sex, out of which, in the end, I emerged as lonely as I began? . . . Although so many boys had passed through my hands I lived with none of them, they came and went, . . . at no point in this journey did I have a feeling of stability, of more than momentary satisfaction.

J. R. ACKERLEY
American writer, 1968

I'm scared to death of what's emerging in the gay middle class. I was at [the New York nightclub] the Saint in costume the other night and I was petrified. I felt like Jezebel when she came into the room with a scarlet dress. No one wanted to go near me. Everyone was so afraid to be different. I call it a gay middle-class vacuum. This conformity is a dangerous thing.

> HIBISCUS
> American performer, 1980s

[On the Mattachine Society, pioneer gay rights group]

We had an initiation ceremony—we'd all hold hands and we had ritualistic things that we said, something like, "No gay person coming into the world will ever again have to feel alone and unwanted and rejected."

> HARRY HAY
> American pioneer activist/writer, 1980s

Someone perfectly alone as a gay person is not gay; he isn't acting as a gay, he isn't even having homosexual sex, except perhaps cautiously, the way many heterosexuals do. He thinks that he is the only person who might be gay, and he probably wouldn't even be thinking *that*—since being the *only* one would mean that he is a monster—so he doesn't have any kind of social identity.

> GUY HOCQUENGHEM
> French activist, 1980s

Wherever I am on this earth, I am, and always shall be, only a resident alien.

> QUENTIN CRISP
> English writer/critic, 1981

[One] misconception is that fathers invariably reject their gay sons. In fact, it is often *the gay son who has rejected the father.*

CHARLES SILVERSTEIN
American writer, 1981

It just isn't true that gay people are lonelier than ungay people (or whatever the opposite of gay is), and I'm in a position to know.

NED ROREM
American composer, 1982

Fact: The Michigan Women's Music Festival announced that male children would not be allowed on festival grounds. Male children over the age of six were to be placed in a camp about ten miles away. . . . I refused to place my Jewish child in a camp because of his undesirability to Lesbian separatists.

SUSAN J. WOLFE
American writer/feminist, 1982

I once wrote about a young man in love. He did not sleep all night, and I listened to his beating heart.

"What is it beating against?" I asked.

"Can't you hear?" said the young man. "It is doing battle with my reason."

It beat as if against the walls of a dungeon, this little, inexperienced, desperate human heart.

DAVID DAR
American writer, 1983

I learned very early in life that I was always going to need people more than they needed me.

> Quentin Crisp
> English writer/critic, 1984

Even with a man whose neck is thicker than his head, if we are not careful, we shall be involved in an argument about who most loves whom. The trouble is that, if you find that by mistake you have bitten into a soft center, you can't very well put it back in the box.

> Quentin Crisp
> English writer/critic, 1984

It's one thing to support Gay Rights. It's another to adore a man you know to be a homosexual, by which you make yourself miserable. By which you make him miserable. It's perverse.

> Barbara Grizzuti Harrison
> American writer, 1984

In 1970 I was 19, gay, and a medic with the Marines in Vietnam. The pain of seeing beautiful men I loved destroyed is still with me. These men stride through my dreams and fantasies. We must never allow another war to waste our brothers and sisters.

> Mike Felker
> Former U.S. Marine, 1984

How many lesbians are in nursing homes or other health-care facilities where they must conceal their identity and live out their lives as strangers in a strange land?

> Monika Kehoe
> American psychologist/writer, 1986

Where are my hard-won ideas about separatism, confrontation, group consciousness? Are we not members of a lost and dispersed tribe, rather than errant offspring?

CARL WITTMAN
American writer/activist, 1980s

While dressing today, I went to Barry's closet and, with a certain amount of relish, took a tie of his. . . . Tying the knot, I knew how handsome he thought me in it—perhaps how handsome I looked to him now, from some cloud—and I wept.

STEPHEN GRECO
American writer, 1987

Our community is experiencing the same kind of devastation that befell the survivors of the world wars. Nothing will alleviate our grief completely, because this tragedy is real and inescapable. But we don't have to cooperate or make it even worse by denying there's an epidemic and refusing to practice safer sex, fragmenting our community by blaming parts of it that we don't like for the disease, or becoming isolated and politically passive.

PAT CALIFIA
American journalist, 1988

[Regarding the first Quilt square designed for his friend, Marvin Feldman]

I spent the whole afternoon thinking about Marvin. I thought about why we were best friends and why I loved him so much. By the time I finished the piece, my grief had been replaced by a sense of resolution and completion. . . .

There's promise in a quilt. It's not a shroud or a tombstone. It's so important for people whose greatest enemy is despair. I really believe that the worst thing that could happen to us is to despair and to stop living and loving and fighting.

CLEVE JONES
American activist/founder of the
NAMES Project, 1988

AIDS has come upon us with cruel abandon. It has forced us to confront and deal with the frailty of our being and the reality of death. It has forced us into a realization that we must cherish every moment of the glorious experience of this thing we call life. We are learning to value our own lives and the lives of our loved ones as if any moment may be the last.

ELIZABETH TAYLOR
American actress, 1988

[Note submitted to NAMES Project with the panel honoring her two sons]

I do hope it's acceptable for me to put the names of both my sons on a single panel. Sydney and Jim would have approved because they were close friends. . . .

I totally accepted the fact of their homosexuality. Unfortunately, the same cannot be said for their father, who is now my ex-husband.

Pray for all of us. I have two more gay sons. I live in fear.

JUDY SOONS
American homemaker, 1988

Of all the groups that suffer discrimination, homosexuals are the loneliest. Black children have black parents, but every homosexual child is an orphan.

Quentin Crisp
English writer/critic, 1988

Sexuality

I n the past it was the concealment that prevented researchers from arriving at the truth about the more intimate aspects of human behavior; now the chief obstacle is the boasting.

In a recent survey a youth was asked how often he engaged in any form of sexual intercourse with a man. "Six times," he replied. The interviewer, writing down his words, murmured, "Six times a week." "No, no," the young man explained. "Six times a night." He seemed mildly amused at the lady's ignorance of her subject.

In spite of constant admonitions not to judge others by ourselves, all our opinions are inevitably based upon our own experience. If we shake hands with someone, we describe his hand as hot if it is warmer than our own, or cold if it is cooler. It is the same with sexual behavior. We term somebody oversexed or undersexed according to whether his performance or even his sexual preoccupations are stronger or feebler than ours.

All the same, whatever standards we apply, it would be difficult to refrain from asking the young man in the interview, "With what object do you pursue sexual experience so vigorously? Toward the end of the evening, it surely cannot continue to be a pleasure."

Since the sexual explosion of the 1950s, it really does seem that the male homosexual community is preoccupied in a schoolboyish fashion not with the quality of its sex life but with the mere number of its *orgasms. This phenomenon arouses suspicion. A person eats an unusually large number of meals a day only if his food contains little or no nutritional value. It is therefore hard not to come to the conclusion that homosexual intercourse among males is unsatisfactory. The fact that this section contains descriptions of sexual antics involving three participants demonstrates incontrovertibly that gay men are forever in search of some phantom superorgasm in a way that lesbians apparently are not.*

With lesbians the lure seems to be softness and sensuality. The sexual processes of women are so subtle and so complicated that it usually takes someone of the same sex to know how to please them.

It is not surprising that the men have such little success in their quest for the superorgasm—they set about it in such a misguided way. They are always trying to engage the attention of the most conventionally good-looking partners—knitwear models with blond hair and blue eyes, as though these attributes had something to do with physical fulfillment. They seem unable to settle for the fact that sex, in whatever form, will provide them with only as much pleasure as their nervous systems can endure.

Blessed is the man who knows how to make love
    as one wrestles in a gym,
and then goes home happy to sleep the day
    with a delicious young boy.

> THEOGNIS
> Greek poet, 6th century B.C.

I, for the sake of that Queen of love, like the wax of the holy bees
that is melted beneath the heat of the sun, waste away when I look
at the young limbs of blooming boys.

> PINDAR
> Greek poet, 522 B.C.–443 B.C.

Men who are slices of the male are followers of the male, and show
their masculinity throughout their boyhood by the way they make
friends with men, and the delight they take in lying beside them and
being taken in their arms. And these are the most hopeful of the
nation's youth, for theirs is the most virile constitution. . . .

And so, when this boy-lover—or any lover, for that matter—is
fortunate enough to meet his other half, they are both so intoxicated
with affection, with friendship, and with love, that they cannot bear
to let each other out of sight for a single instant. It is such reunions
as these that impel men to spend their lives together, although they
may be hard put to say what they really want with one another; and
indeed, the purely sexual pleasures of their friendship could hardly
account for the huge delight they take in one another's company.

> PLATO
> Greek philosopher, 427? B.C.–347 B.C.

Neglect your Guard, and let him get the best;
Then he'll be mild, then you a Kiss may seize,
He'll struggle, but at length comply with ease;
Reluctant, tho' at first you'll find him grow
Ev'n fond, when round your Neck his Arms he'll throw.

> TIBULLUS
> Roman poet
> c. 60 and 48 B.C.–19 B.C.

[Comment regarding homosexuality among Celtic males of the period]

Although they have good-looking women, they pay very little attention to them, but are really crazy about having sex with men. They
are accustomed to sleep on the ground on animal skins and roll
around with male bedmates on both sides. Heedless of their own
dignity, they abandon without a qualm the bloom of their bodies to
others. And the most incredible thing is that they don't think this is
shameful. But when they proposition someone, they consider it dis-
honorable if he doesn't accept the offer!

> DIODORUS SICULUS
> Roman historian, 20 B.C.

Count as three all those on a bed, of whom two are active
And two are passive. I seem to relate a marvel,
Yet it is not a falsehood: the one in the middle performs doubly,
Pleasing in the back and being pleased in the front.

> STRATO
> Greek philosopher
> c. A.D. 2

Love is beautiful and decorous; pleasure is vulgar and servile. For this reason it is considered uncouth for a free man to be in love with slaves, since this sort of passion is merely sexual, like relations with women.

> PLUTARCH
> Greek biographer/essayist, 46?–120

Men, leaving the natural use of the woman, burned in their lust one toward another.

> THE BIBLE
> From St. Paul's Epistle to the Romans, 1:26

Thus I contaminated the spring of friendship with the dirt of lust and darkened its brightness with the blackness of desire.

> ST. AUGUSTINE OF HIPPO
> Early Christian Church father/philosopher
> 354–430

A boy is for pleasure; a woman for children.

> Persian proverb
> 800

"But humans should not be like birds or pigs:
Humans have reason.
Peasants, who may as well be called pigs—
These are the only men who should resort to women."

> ANONYMOUS
> Medieval poet, 1120?
> Ganymede, in "Ganymede and Helen"

You are the common desire of lasses and lads;
They sigh for you and hope for you because they know you are
    unique.

> HILARY THE ENGLISHMAN
> English poet, 1150?

Venus kindles all fires, but the greatest heat
Is in sex with males; whoever has tried it knows it.

> ANONYMOUS
> Medieval monk, 1150?

Alas, how can a love that's chaste
(Such as burns now so strongly within me),
Be seen by him whose love is otherwise?

> MICHELANGELO BUONARROTI
> Italian sculptor/painter/architect/poet
> 1475–1564

Tell me, dearest, what is love?
'T is a lightning from above;
'T is an arrow, 't is a fire,
'T is a boy they call desire.

> FRANCIS BEAUMONT (1584–1616)
> AND JOHN FLETCHER (1579–1625)

I storm and I roar, and I fall in a rage,
And missing my Whore, I bugger my Page.

> JOHN WILMOT,
> EARL OF ROCHESTER
> English poet, 1647–1680

Buggery we chose and Buggery we allow
For none but fops alone to cunts will bow.

> JOHN WILMOT,
> EARL OF ROCHESTER
> English poet, 1648–1680

In England the vices in fashion are whoring and drinking, in Turkey,
Sodomy & smoking. We prefer a girl and a bottle, they a pipe and
a pathic.—They are sensible people.

> LORD BYRON
> English poet, 1788–1824

For boyish minions of unhallowed love
The shameless torch of wild desire is lit,
Caressed, preferred even to women's self above,
Whose forms for Nature's gentler errors fit
All frailties mote excuse save that which they commit.

> LORD BYRON
> English poet, 1788–1824

O my body! I dare not desert the likes of you in other men and
   women, nor the likes of the parts of you,
I believe the likes of you are to stand or fall with the likes of the soul
   (and that they are the soul).

> WALT WHITMAN
> American poet, 1819–1892

Little you know the subtle electric fire that for
   your sake is playing within me.

> WALT WHITMAN
> American poet, 1819–1892

I mind how once we lay such a transparent summer morning,
How you settled your head athwart my hips and gently turn'd over
　　upon me.
And parted the shirt from my bosom-bone, and plunged your tongue
　　to my bare-stript heart,
And reach'd till you felt my beard, and reach'd till you held my
　　feet.

WALT WHITMAN
American poet, 1819–1892

You give me the pleasure of your eyes, face, flesh, as we pass—you
take of my beard, breast, hands, in return.

WALT WHITMAN
American poet, 1819–1892

The sin we had done once, and with loathing, we would do many
times, and with joy.

OSCAR WILDE
Irish writer, 1854–1900

Erection: A word used only when speaking of monuments.

GUSTAVE FLAUBERT
French novelist, 1821–1880

Dark and wrinkled like a deep pink,
It breathes, humbly nestled among the moss
Still wet with love.

PAUL VERLAINE
French poet, 1844–1896
From "Sonnet to an Asshole"

Tender, the young auburn woman,
  By such innocence aroused,
Said to the blonde young girl
  These words, in a soft low voice:

"Sap which mounts, and flowers which thrust,
  Your childhood is a bower:
Let my fingers wander in the moss
  Where glows the rosebud."

PAUL VERLAINE
French poet, 1844–1896

I spent the night between two fellows from the docks,
Who took turns, and cured me of the hots!

JEAN LORRAIN
(Pseudonym for Paul Duval)
French journalist, 1850–1906

No civilized man ever regrets a pleasure, and no uncivilized man ever knows what a pleasure is.

OSCAR WILDE
Irish writer, 1854–1900

An inordinate passion for pleasure is the secret of remaining young.

OSCAR WILDE
Irish writer, 1854–1900
From *Lord Arthur Savile's Crime*

A kiss may ruin a human life.

> OSCAR WILDE
> Irish writer, 1854–1900
> From *A Woman of No Importance*

"I have never searched for happiness. Who wants happiness? I have searched for pleasure."
"And found it, Mr. Gray?"
"Often. Too often."

> OSCAR WILDE
> Irish writer, 1854–1900
> Dorian Gray, in *The Picture of Dorian Gray*

The popular theory of the sexual instinct corresponds closely to the poetic fable of dividing the person into two halves—man and woman—who strive to become reunited through love. It is, therefore, very surprising to find that there are men for whom the sexual object is not woman but man, and that there are women for whom it is not man but woman. Such *persons* are designated as contrary sexuals, or better, inverts, and the situation of such a relationship is called inversion. The number of such individuals is considerable, although it is difficult to estimate them accurately.

> SIGMUND FREUD
> Austrian neurologist/founder of
> psychoanalysis, 1856–1939

[When asked her opinion of homosexual affairs replied]

I don't care what people do, as long as they don't do it in the street and frighten the horses!

> MRS. PATRICK CAMPBELL
> English actress, 1865–1940

They burned with each other, inwardly. This they would never admit. They intended to keep their relationship a casual free-and-easy friendship, they were not going to be so unmanly and unnatural as to allow any heart-burning between them. They had not the faintest belief in deep relationship between men and men, and their disbelief prevented any development of their powerful but suppressed friendliness.

D. H. LAWRENCE
English novelist/poet/painter, 1885–1930
Description of Gerald and Birkin, in
Women in Love

On their first day in St. Louis, Bessie entered the room shared by Ruby and Lillian. She walked up behind Lillian, leaned forward, and kissed her.

Embarrassed, Lillian looked at Ruby and jerked away. "Don't play around with me like that," she said.

Bessie grabbed her around the waist. "Is that how you feel?"

"Yes!" Lillian said. "That's exactly how I feel."

"The hell with you, bitch," said Bessie. "I got twelve women on this show and I can have one every night if I want it. Don't you feel so important, and don't you say another word to me while you're on this show, or I'll send you home bag and baggage."

RUBY WALKER
American performer/Bessie Smith's niece
1927

I know women that don't like men
The way they do is a crying sin.
It's dirty but good, oh, yes, it's dirty but good
There ain't much difference, it's just dirty but good.

BESSIE SMITH
American singer, 1894–1937
From "It's Dirty But Good"

Every farmer who has raised cattle knows . . . that cows quite regularly mount cows.

> ALFRED KINSEY
> American zoologist/sociologist/sexologist
> 1894–1956

Don't you know of same-gender heterosexual friendships in which there's a strong attraction? It doesn't have to be sexual to be romantic.

> GEORGE CUKOR
> American film director, 1899–1983

Today it's all sex, no romance. All blatant and untextured.

> CECIL BEATON
> British photographer/writer/designer
> 1902–1980

Do you know that in ancient Greek there was no word for homosexuality? Because there is just . . . to be *sexual*. One is not this or that, one is *sexual*.

> LUCHINO VISCONTI
> Italian film director, 1906–1976

For a man to have sex with another man is to become doubly a man.

> JEAN GENET
> French playwright/writer, 1910–1986

Men who don't fall in love but just go for one-night stands and bar pickups, they get wolfish looking, you can see it in their eyes. Their eyes lose a certain . . . humanity, because they only want the brutal sexual act.

TENNESSEE WILLIAMS
American playwright, 1912–1983

Seventy-five percent of our time at least is spent on lesbians.

WILLIAM MASTERS
American sexologist

I just closed my eyes and thought of England.

[Comment regarding his controversial on-screen kiss with actor Murray Head in the film *Sunday, Bloody Sunday*, directed by John Schlesinger]

PETER FINCH
English actor, 1916–1977

"Liberace's Hot Nuts"

LIBERACE
American musician/entertainer, 1919–1987
Inscription on glass nut bowls sold at the
auction of his estate

The good thing about masturbation is that you don't have to dress up for it.

TRUMAN CAPOTE
American writer, 1924–1984

Your hand trembles in mine
Like a frightened pigeon. I fear
Your pink beak will peck
My youth, the sole fruit I have.

> YUKIO MISHIMA
> Japanese novelist, 1925–1970

What the gay movement needs now is much more the art of life than a science or scientific knowledge (or pseudoscientific knowledge) of what sexuality is. Sexuality is a part of our behavior. It's a part of our world freedom. . . . Sex is not a fatality; it is a possibility for creative life.

> MICHEL FOUCAULT
> French author/philosopher, 1926–1984

[Comment made to Senator Briggs citing statistics that indicated that the average gay man has over five hundred sexual contacts]

I wish.

> HARVEY MILK
> American politician/activist, 1930–1978

How many painful disillusions would be saved if, instead of thinking themselves obliged to say "I love you," men would content themselves with saying "I desire you."

> RENÉ GUYON
> French writer/activist, 1934

The Greek symbolizes ancient sex . . . and homosexuality—uninhibited sexuality and wonderful bodies.

RAINER WERNER FASSBINDER
German film director, 1946–1982

Sexual energy not used by homosexuals for procreation, as it is by heterosexuals, should be channelized elsewhere where its ends can be creativity.

HARRY HAY
American activist, 1951

Sex is. There is nothing more to be done about it. Sex builds no roads, writes no novels and sex certainly gives no meaning to anything in life but itself.

GORE VIDAL
American writer, 1960

The sailor who stands against a wall, looking down at the bobbing head of the gobbling queen, regards himself as master of the situation; yet it is the queen (does not that derisive epithet suggest primacy and dominion?) who has won the day, extracting from the flesh of the sailor his posterity, the one element in every man which is eternal (a scientific fact) and cellularly resembles not at all the rest of the body.

GORE VIDAL
American writer, 1968
Myra Breckinridge, in *Myra Breckinridge*

Our culture has resolutely resisted the idea of bisexuality. We must insist that there is only one *right* way of having sex: man and woman joined together to make baby; all else is wrong.

GORE VIDAL
American writer, 1968
Myra Breckinridge, in *Myra Breckinridge*

The ass is the face of the soul of sex.

CHARLES BUKOWSKI
American writer, 1969

There will be sex after death, we just won't be able to feel it.

LILY TOMLIN
American actress/comedian, 1970s

What is the ultimate sexual rejection?

Having your hand fall asleep while you're masturbating.

American joke, 1970s

Conventional heterosexual intercourse is like squirting jam into a doughnut.

GERMAINE GREER
Australian author, 1970s

It's too bad that every male cannot have instruction from a female homosexual prior to marriage. Only a female homosexual really knows how to make love to a woman. We, as men, are kind of duds along those lines.

EARLE M. MARCH
American sexologist, 1972

The cues that a woman receives from another woman are more subtle than the cues men give each other. . . . Two women do not have to explain away an erection should one of them get excited while they were having a tête-à-tête and talking about their sex lives.

PEPPER SCHWARTZ AND
PHILIP BLUMSTEIN
American sexologists, 1973

INTERVIEWER: Was your first sexual experience with a man or a woman?

GORE VIDAL: I was much too polite to ask.

GORE VIDAL
American writer, 1973
From an interview in *Viva* magazine

Voyeurism is a healthy, non-participatory sexual activity—the world *should* look at the world.

DESMOND MORRIS
English zoologist, 1974

Bisexuality immediately doubles your chances for a date on Saturday night.

WOODY ALLEN
American writer/director/actor, 1975

When you sleep with somebody younger you do gain a little vitality of breadth and bounce.

ALLEN GINSBERG
American poet, 1975

I don't think there's anything wrong with relating to people on the level of pure meat, as long as you don't get trapped into that all the time as a single level of consciousness—as some queens do.

ALLEN GINSBERG
American poet, 1975

Hey, don't knock masturbation. It's sex with someone I love.

WOODY ALLEN
American writer/director/actor, 1977
From *Annie Hall*

Bath sign language predates Noel Coward. The signals are the same throughout the world. Examples? If one's towel is knotted in the back, sodomy is the order of the night. Lying on one's back on a cot, legs ajar, is an open call for fellatio. And one doesn't have to be an Einstein to know what lying on one's stomach means.

ARTHUR BELL
American writer, 1977

There is no middle class sexual style for men. What would it be based on? Golfing? Discussing stock options? Attending church? Downing highballs?

> EDMUND WHITE
> American novelist/essayist, 1979

I've been told we live in a sex-ridden society. I would have said that we live in a world corroded with envy.

> QUENTIN CRISP
> English writer/critic, 1979

Until more is known about the origins of heterosexuality it is difficult to believe that meaningful insights will be reached regarding the origins of homosexuality.

> WILLIAM MASTERS AND
> VIRGINIA JOHNSON
> American sexologists, 1979

The idea of sex with a man doesn't turn me off, but I don't express it. I satisfied my curiosity about that years ago. I had lots of sex between the ages of three and four and the time I was fourteen or fifteen. Strange experiences with older boys. But men don't particularly turn me on. And, no, John [Oates] and I have never been lovers. He's not my type. Too short and dark.

> DARYL HALL
> American rock musician, 1980s

The big mistake that men make is that when they turn thirteen or fourteen and all of a sudden they've reached puberty, they believe that they like women. Actually, you're just horny. It doesn't mean you like women any more at twenty-one than you did at ten.

JULES FEIFFER
American cartoonist/writer, 1980

Sexual freedom has become more important than identity. Indeed, it has superseded it. The modern philosophy states, "I ejaculate, therefore I am."

QUENTIN CRISP
English writer/critic, 1981

The man who *never* has sex with someone a second time, no matter how enjoyable it was, is essentially saying that the conquest—the seduction—is more gratifying than the genital experience itself—a position, it seems to me, typical of sexual aggression, rather than of sexual love.

CHARLES SILVERSTEIN
American writer, 1981

It's absolutely lovely that friends go to bed with each other now, heterosexually or homosexually. But I'm still excited by the anonymous.

NED ROREM
American composer, 1982

Come forth, come forth, at least once every day!

JAMES BROUGHTON
American poet/playwright/filmmaker, 1982

The clone—the gay everyman—is vitally concerned with sexual expression.

> John Preston
> American writer, 1983

Sex with strangers is an alternative to language, the code that replaces speech.

> Edmund White
> American novelist/essayist, 1983

If you ask a homosexual what his newest true love is like, you will never get the answer "He is wise or kind or brave." He will only say, "It's enormous."

> Quentin Crisp
> English writer/critic, 1984

At one time I imagined my sexual abnormality constituted the whole of my difference from other people; later I decided that the rift was caused by my exalted views on love. Finally I saw that these two causes were interdependent. Universal love goes with masturbation.

> Quentin Crisp
> English writer/critic, 1984

Bedrooms are a place to sleep, to dream, to love. The gay male does not, however, confine himself only to bedrooms as they are designated in buildings by architects. His bedroom is of a movable kind. Where one can sleep, dream, and love, there is his bedroom.

> Timothy Murphy
> American journalist/professor of medical
> ethics, 1985

Bringing guests home for sex is usually not advisable, even in a very open relationship. No matter how passionately two lovers pledge undying fidelity to one another, the unexpected presence of a third attractive body usually provides enough tinder to set off an emotional firestorm that makes the burning of Troy look like a quiet marshmallow roast.

BRYAN MONTE
American writer/editor, 1986

In an enlightened culture to confine sex to procreative heterosexual monogamy is archaic.

PHIL NASH
American writer/activist, 1986

Sexuality and self-esteem go together.

SARA CYTRON
American comedian, 1988

Public sex is a problem that gay men are largely responsible for perpetuating and one that gay activists should not shunt. Besides the risk of arrest and danger of violence to those involved, public sex makes all gay men look bad in the eyes of the average American bigot. And, frankly, it's something that users of public facilities should not have to be exposed to—nor should their children.

DAVE WALTER
American journalist, 1988

[Observations of dolphin behavior]

There'll be a group of four of five males, and it seems like one of them goes, "Let's get Pointer!" And the other males start mounting him with erections. . . . The males are constantly mounting each other.

RICHARD CONNOR
American scientist, 1988

Watching safe-sex videos is like . . . watching professional football players play touch. People don't want that.

PERRY ROSS
American video merchandiser/officer of the
Adult Video Association, 1988

I'm scared to death of the individual who has no sexual desires, no romantic desires, no fantasies.

JOHN CARDINAL O'CONNOR
Roman Catholic Archbishop of New York
1988

SUBJECT INDEX